Climbing Mastery:
Practical Exercises for Technique and Strength Training

Unlock Your Climbing Potential with Effective Training Methods

Copyright © 2023

All rights reserved. No part of this work covered by the copyright herein may be reproduced

CONTENTS

INTRODUCTION
THE 10 COMMANDMENTS OF CLIMBING

WARMING UP

THE WARM-UP PROGRAMME

CHAPTER 1: TECHNIQUE

FOOTWORK

GRIP POSITIONS

BALANCE

TENSION & DIRECTION OF FORCE

DYNAMICS

TRICKS

COMBINATION EXERCISES

TRAINING FOR TRAD & ALPINE – by Martine Limstrand

CHAPTER 2: STRENGTH & POWER

EXERCISES ON THE WALL

IMPORTANT CONSIDERATIONS FOR GETTING THE MOST OUT OF YOUR STRENGTH TRAINING

STRENGTH EXERCISES

POSITIONING EXERCISES

POWER EXERCISES

ISOLATED STRENGTH EXERCISES

EXERCISES USING A PORTABLE FINGERBOARD

ARM & UPPER BODY STRENGTH EXERCISES

VARIATION IN TRAINING – by Tina Johnsen Hafsaas

CHAPTER 3: CHILDREN & YOUTHS

WARMING UP FOR CHILDREN

CLIMBING GAMES

TECHNIQUE EXERCISES

TRAVERSING

STRENGTH TRAINING FOR CHILDREN & YOUTHS

WHY SHOULD CHILDREN & YOUTHS TRAIN STRENGTH?

HOW SHOULD CHILDREN & YOUTHS TRAIN STRENGTH?

PHOTO: RYAN WATERS
'FOR MANY YEARS I DIDN'T TRAIN, I JUST CLIMBED. IT TOOK YEARS FOR ME TO REALISE I HAD TO TRAIN TO IMPROVE.'

Joakim Louis Sæther sends *Crassostrea Gigas* (F8b, trad), Bohuslän, Sweden.

INTRODUCTION

'IN THEORY THERE'S NO DIFFERENCE BETWEEN THEORY AND PRACTICE. IN PRACTICE THERE IS.'

AFTER TWO DECADES of climbing, training and coaching we have built up a large and ever-growing library of exercises. This Book was a large project where we wanted to include the different performance factors and the underlying theory, which resulted in us having to limit the selection of exercises due to lack of space. Therefore, in the back of our minds we knew that we had to write the book as well which you now have in your hands.

This book focuses on technique, strength and power, as we wanted to explore these topics further to create variation in and new challenges for your training. Endurance, flexibility and the mental aspects are left out as we feel these are explained in enough detail in *The Climbing Bible*. In this book, chapter 1 describes exercises to improve anything from the precision of your footwork to long dynos, while chapter 2 features exercises to train specific strength and power. We hope this book will end up with its pages filled with chalk marks and its cover worn out after living in your gym bag. Our recommendation is that you carry it with you and try at least one new exercise in every training session.

In addition to inspiring both young and old to vary their training, we wish to help parents and coaches create great sessions and make kids even more psyched for climbing. As Stian says, happiness is seeing your children find the same joy in climbing as you do yourself. Chapter 3 therefore features games, technique exercises and physical training ideas for children.

THE 10 COMMANDMENTS OF CLIMBING

PHOTO: BJØRNAR SMESTAD
Stian Christophersen climbing in the 2019 National Lead finals in Oslo, Norway.

1. You have to climb a lot to become a good climber.

2. Vary your climbing between different styles and angles – both indoors and outdoors.

3. Train technique before physical training.

4. Learn to use your feet – they will be your best friends on the wall.

5. Rid yourself of your fear of falling.

6. Train finger strength.

7. Find your strengths and weaknesses, set yourself targets and adapt your training accordingly.

8. What and how you think is critical to your success – become just as strong mentally as you are physically and technically.

9. Create – or become part of – a supportive and challenging community.

10. Preserve the joy – climbing is all fun and games.

WARMING UP

WHY SHOULD I WARM UP?

WARMING UP PREPARES us to perform physically, technically and mentally, and also reduces our risk of injury. The warm-up should consist of a general part and a specific part. The general part can include running, jumping, push-ups, squats and similar activities, with the goal being to activate the whole body and to use the larger muscle groups. The warm-up is also a good time to incorporate some injury prevention exercises, where you can practise movement patterns that are the opposite of what you'll face when climbing. For youths and adults the general part should last for at least 10 minutes, while it should last a little while longer for children – for at least 20 minutes.

The specific part should be climbing based. The most common approach is to start with some easy climbing on good holds, before progressing to increasingly harder climbing. For this part of the warm-up you can – and should – add technical elements that you wish to work on. To properly warm up your fingers to reduce the risk of injury, it is recommended that you do over 100 moves during your warm-up and before you increase the level of difficulty. Your warm-up should also be specifically targeted towards whatever the main part of your training session will consist of. If you're going to do steep bouldering, the last part of your specific warm-up should consist of steep moves to make sure that your arms, upper body and core muscles are properly warmed up and ready. If you're going to do vertical lead climbing, your warm-up should reflect this, by focusing on warming up your fingers and adding in hip-mobility exercises. In addition to preparing yourself physically, warming up will also mentally prepare you for performing. Having the specific part of your warm-up resemble what you'll be doing in the main part of your session will have a positive effect on how well prepared you will be mentally for what is about to happen.

Begin with easy traversing on good holds or some easy top-roping. Then progress to more dynamic moves. One simple exercise is to double-dyno between good holds while keeping your feet on the wall. Remember that climbing is all about fun and freedom of movement, so try to let loose mentally and climb dynamically, playing around with dynos, to get some flow in your movement. In our experience, many climbers are more agile during the main part of their session if they take this approach during their warm-up.

THE WARM-UP PROGRAMME

GENERAL PART

Start your warm-up by activating your blood circulation and larger muscle groups. For example, you can use a skipping rope, go for a run, or walk or run up some stairs. To activate your upper body you can add in some burpees in sets of 10. Alternate between these variants for about 10 minutes, and you'll be ready to move on with the following exercises:

COSSACK SQUATS: Complete one set of ten repetitions to each side.

STANDING ROTATIONS: Complete one set of ten repetitions to each side.

THORACIC BRIDGE: Complete one set of five repetitions to each side.

SPECIFIC PART

As mentioned earlier, we recommend completing at least 100 moves during your warm-up, independent of what you will be training afterwards, and this is best accomplished on a rope or by traversing the bouldering wall. During this part of your warm-up you have the opportunity to practise clipping technique, footwork, resting and dynamic moves. The last part of the specific warm-up should resemble what you'll focus on during your main training session. We have included suggestions here for exercises to do before your most intensive sessions, where you'll need some extra warming up before you're ready to really start training.

PULL-UPS:

During your warm-up we recommend that you drop all the way down until your arms are straight and start the pulling motion by pulling your shoulder blades down and together, rotating your elbows in towards each other and steadily pulling up through the whole movement. Complete three sets of five repetitions. Use an elastic band or a pulley system to take some of the load off, to ensure it's an actual warm-up and not strength training.

POWER PULL-UPS:

Use an elastic band and complete four to six pull-ups where you generate as much speed as possible when pulling up. If you're going to be bouldering or climbing hard you can add some high-speed pull-ups at the end of your warm-up to activate the upper body musculature.

DEADHANGS:

Use a pulley system to take some of the load off. Complete five sets of 5- to 10-second hangs using different grip positions (for example, open hand, half crimp, three-finger open, and so on).

KICK STARTS:

Start with one hand and one foot on the wall and spring from the floor to catch a hold on the wall with your free hand. Complete six different-length kick starts for each arm, varying the holds.

JUMP TO EDGE OR HOLD:

Jump to and grab a one- or two-handed hold. Complete six jumps in total and vary the hold type and distance to the hold/s.

CHAPTER 1
TECHNIQUE

AFTER READING THE *Climbing Bible* you'll be familiar with the fundamentals which underlie all climbing movement. You should also know which specific techniques you can use to move around on the wall in a controlled and efficient manner. In this chapter we cover different exercises to train these fundamentals and specific techniques. We also show you efficient exercises for training footwork and grip positions. We begin with the easiest exercises and move on to gradually more challenging ones, so start working on your technique with the first one and work your way up from there.

Before you begin, we want to repeat some of the most important things you should keep in mind when practising technique. First and foremost, it is important that you reserve some of your training sessions – where you are rested and motivated to learn – for focusing only on technique. These exercises require you to concentrate, so avoid practising technique when you are tired. You can practise technique in the same sessions as when you train strength or endurance, but it should always come before the hard physical training.

You should also have separate focus areas for each session. For optimal progression it is important to target what you feel are your weaknesses as a climber. However, you should further develop what you are already good at as well, so continue to cultivate your strengths while working on your weaknesses. If you're unsure of your strengths and weaknesses, you can ask a climbing partner or get help from an experienced coach.

When the session starts, it's important that you have a sense of how the exercise should be carried out and how you're performing it. By first observing others and then filming yourself while doing the exercise, it will be easier for you to get a sense for how you're doing and get direct feedback on your performance. If you also have someone you can discuss the exercise with, the chances of learning will be greater. A climbing partner with more experience than yourself or an experienced climbing coach are the best people with which to discuss the exercise.

INTENSITY

In most sports, athletes train technique at low intensity levels. In climbing, however, we have a tendency to always try our hardest to top a boulder problem or route in every single session. This is not optimal! By conducting specific sessions at lower intensities and focusing on proper execution, you'll soon become much better at moving around on the wall.

PHOTO: STIAN CHRISTOPHERSEN
Joakim Louis Sæther on *Maraton*, Norway's first F8b. *Maraton* is located at the Demperhylla sector at Damtjern. The crag is known for vertical walls, small holds and technically demanding climbing.

FOOTWORK

YOUR LEGS AND feet can and should take a large part of the load that is necessary to keep you on the wall. To be able to do this, you need to be precise when placing your feet on the holds to ensure that they don't slip off, and you should lower your body such that as much of your weight as possible is distributed on to your feet and off of your upper body. The following pages feature some exercises to target exactly this.

PHOTO: PETTER SLUNGAARD KRISTENSEN
Jarl Gåsvær sending *Storpillaren* (N7, approx. E5 6a) on Vågakallen, Lofoten, Norway.

CHOOSING SHOES

As a general rule, you shouldn't wear worn-out shoes when working on refining your footwork. Trusting your feet is something that will come naturally when you're actually standing on holds that you consider difficult to stand on; the likelihood of this happening with worn-out shoes isn't great. On the following pages we highlight the advantages of soft or stiff shoes where choosing one or the other has an impact on the exercise, but for most of the exercises any good all-round shoe will do.

LOOK UP – LOOK DOWN

Many climbers, especially beginners, forget to look at where they are placing their feet. Therefore, make it a rule to always look down at your foot when you're placing it on a hold. It's important that you do not look up before you have actually placed your foot exactly where you want it. When your foot is in place you can look up and move to the next handhold. Your gaze should therefore alternate up and down every time you move a foot or a hand. Try climbing a route where you consistently move your gaze to the foot or hand about to be moved. If you forget, reverse the move and do it again.

 This can quickly become rather pumpy, so begin with routes well within your ability level.

BABY STEPS
To help practise your footwork, try making three moves with your feet for

every individual hand move. This is perhaps unnecessary to climb a route or a boulder problem, but it's a good way to practise precision footwork and it makes you more aware of how important it is to actually look at your feet when you are placing them on a foothold. It's a good idea to start with routes with large footholds before progressing to smaller and smaller holds.

 It can be a good idea to choose lines on the wall with multiple routes as this way you can choose to use footholds from another route if necessary.

HIGH STEPS
As a climber, you're bound to come across high steps, so you might as well start practising them from the get-go. To practise efficiently, choose a route you can do quite easily and place your feet as high as you can for every move. High steps require flexibility, but it's possible to cheat your

way up by moving your hips out and away from the wall, as long as the handholds are good enough. However, climbing on slopers inhibits you from moving your hips too far out from the wall and therefore forces you to work on hip mobility when placing your feet high.

 Stiffer shoes are better when doing high steps to small footholds.

DOWNCLIMBING

Downclimbing forces you to look at your feet when you are placing them, so try climbing up a route and then back down again. Pair up with a climbing partner and alternate who climbs and who belays. You can also do this session on an auto belay, but this isn't ideal, as the auto belay is constantly pulling upwards while you're downclimbing.

 Start with easy, vertical routes which are well within your limit as downclimbing is more pumpy than you might think.

NINJA FEET

Try climbing a route or boulder problem that's well within your limit and without making a sound when placing your feet on the footholds. To be able to do this, you will need to look at your feet and be very precise when placing them on the holds. This will also train your balance, as you will need to be in a position that gives you enough time to place your feet properly and with precision.

If you find placing your feet precisely and silently difficult, instead try practising while still on the ground. Choose different footholds near the ground – preferably holds with different shapes – and practise placing one foot while keeping the other on the ground. Keep your balance by holding on to holds on the wall with your hands as this mimics the situation you'll face while actually climbing.

 Use softer shoes to begin with as it's easier to precisely place a softer shoe. They also make less sound, as the softer rubber more easily conforms to the shape of the holds.

STICKY FEET

On many footholds there might be only the tiniest of grooves in which to place your foot. When placing your foot on these holds there's little room to adjust your foot after placing it. This means you have to be very precise when placing the tip of your shoe on the hold. To practise this, you can climb routes where you don't allow yourself to move or twist your foot to either side once it is placed on a hold.

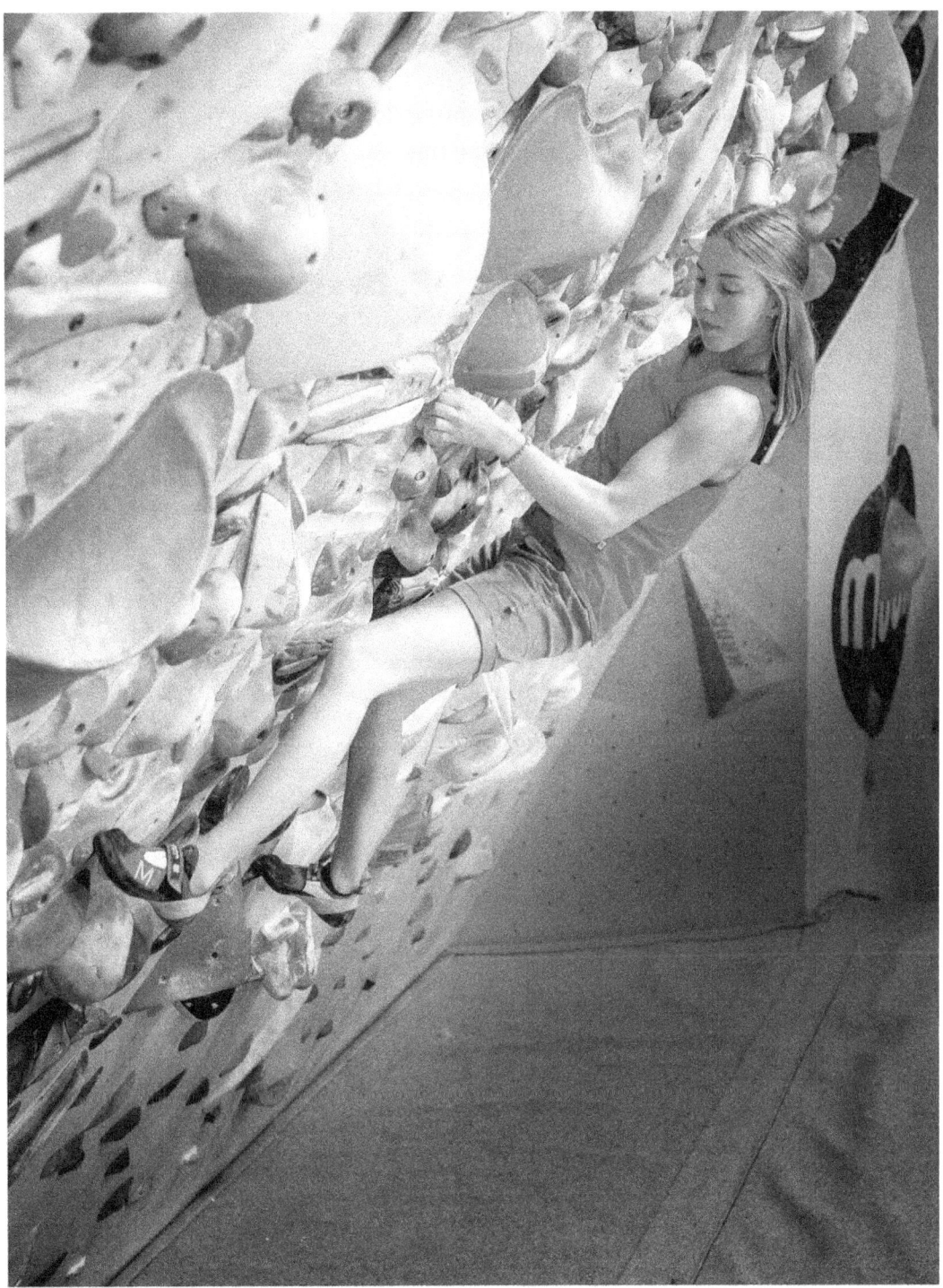

CHIPS ONLY
The style of route setting in climbing walls differs from one to the other,

but if you have the option to climb routes with small screw-on footholds or chips only, this is a really good way to train precision footwork.[*] Standing on small footholds demands even more precision to hit that tiny dimple or protrusion.

[*] Chips are those small holds set with regular wood screws instead of bolts like normal holds, and intended to be used exclusively as footholds. Also known as foot dinks, jibs or just screw-ons.

Use your creativity and climb routes where you only use the small footholds (if this is an option). You could also choose to stand only on the tiny dimple on the side of a larger hold, or all the way to the left or right on a larger edge, for example.

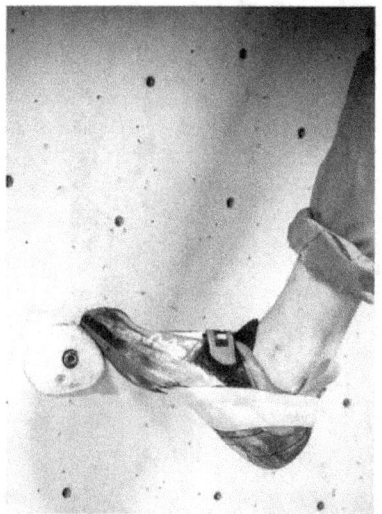 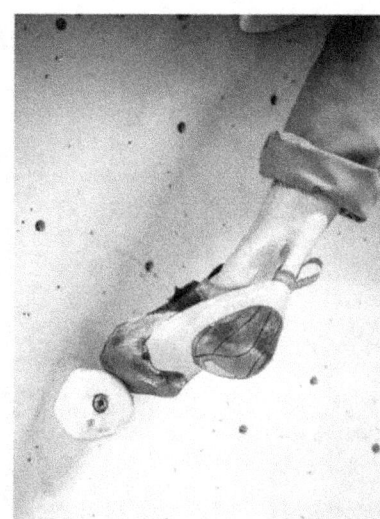 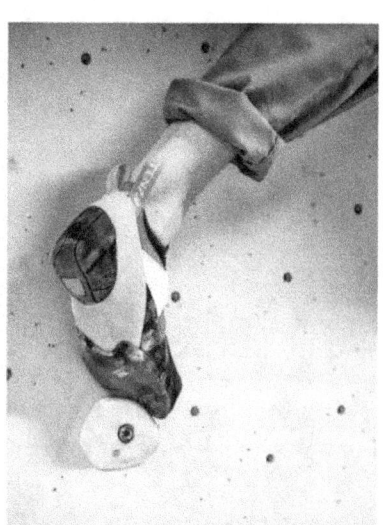

How to place your foot correctly.

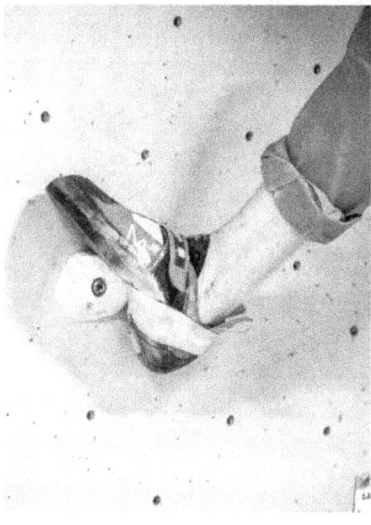 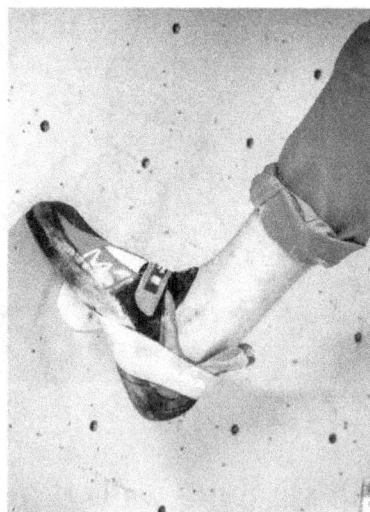 

Your foot can twist off the hold when placed incorrectly.

USE THE TIP

Rookie climbers will tend to place the middle of their foot on a foothold. This is unfortunate as a climbing shoe loses many of its properties when placed in this way. In addition to your climbing being less precise, you will lose the ability to twist your body around the foothold without your foot slipping off the hold. In most cases you should use the tip of your shoe to stand on footholds. You will sometimes use the sides of the shoe, but even then it's still the inside or outside edge of the tip of the shoe which you're using.

A good exercise for practising this is to traverse a wall with lots of holds and observe what happens when you place the inside or outside of your foot on the hold, and not the tip. In many cases you'll fall when you move on as your foot will twist off the hold.

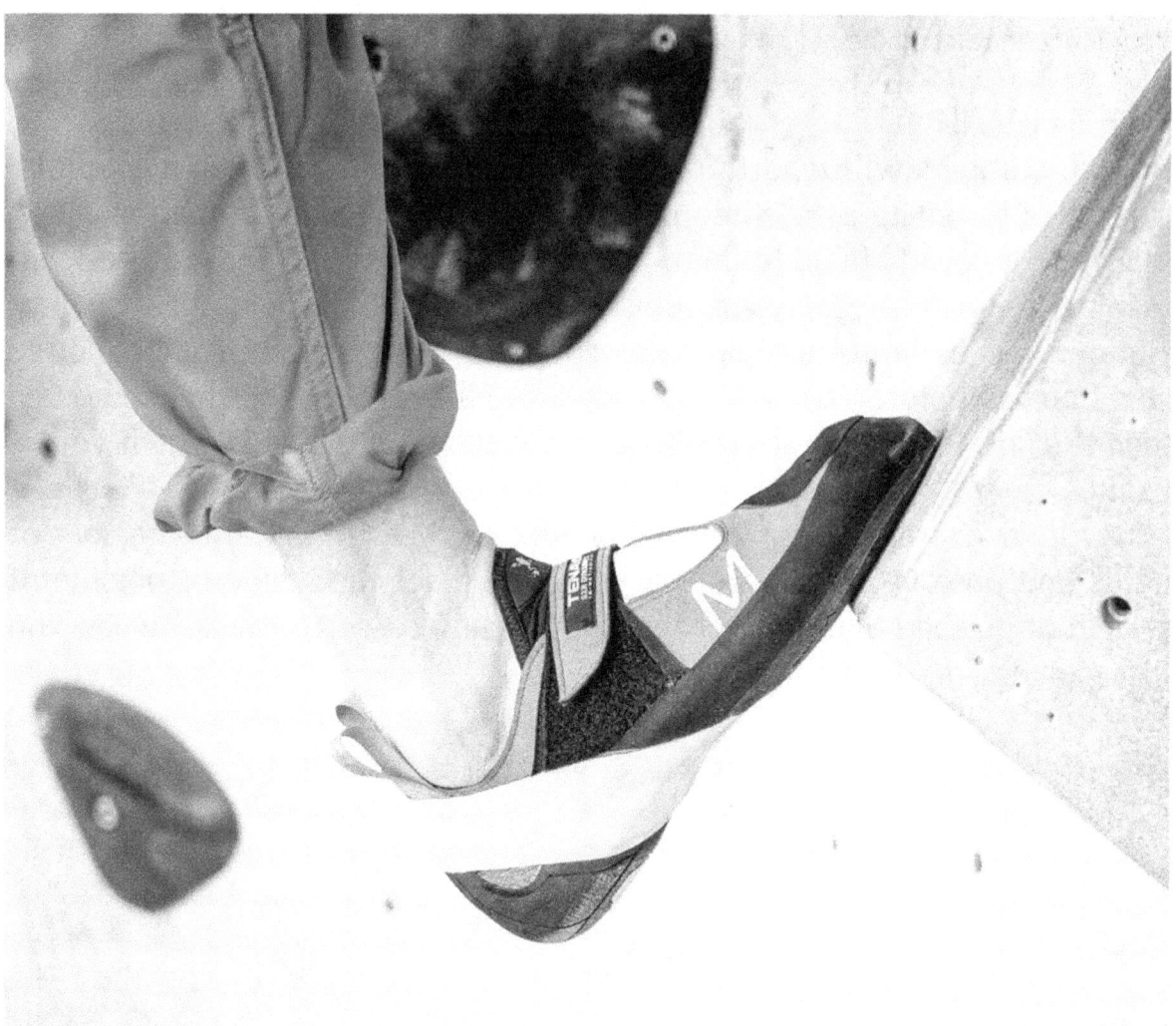

INTERMEDIATE STEPS

In order to stand securely on slopey holds, volumes and walls it's important to be able to smear your feet on the holds. And to smear on the footholds you need to lower your heel to maximise the contact surface between the shoe and the hold/wall. A good way to practise this is to stand directly on to the wall (i.e. not on a foothold) with one foot before placing your other foot on the next foothold. Choose routes or boulder problems well within your limit and only use walls with friction. If the walls in your gym are smoothly painted, it'll be near impossible to complete this exercise. If this is the case, you can try to do the same exercise every time there's a volume on the route or boulder problem. There's usually always friction on these.

To understand the importance of lowering your heel, try playing around with a couple of good handholds and a wall with friction: start with your arms straight and your heel lowered. Then pull up with your arms and notice how as your heel lifts the chance of your foot slipping increases.

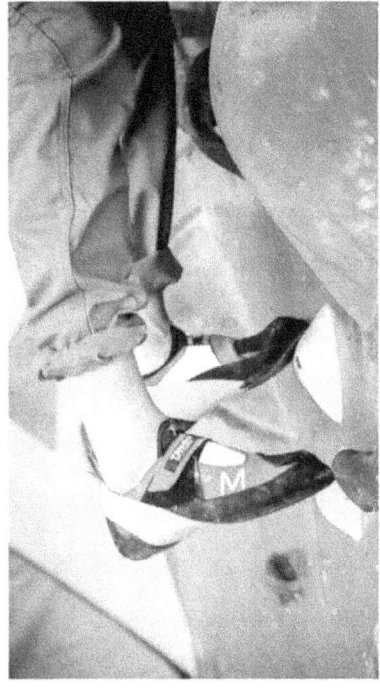  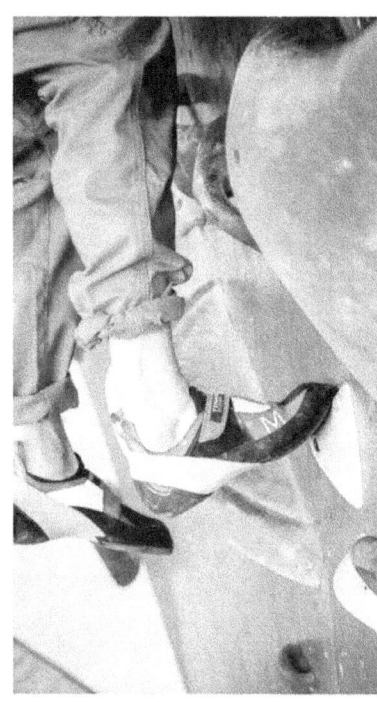

MATCHING FEET

When climbing, you'll often need to match your feet, which means switching your feet on the same foothold. This is an important technique, particularly when traversing. There are several ways to match your feet. If the hold is relatively large, you can place one foot to the side so that there's enough room for your other foot as well. This doesn't require more than a bit of planning and simple precision. If there's not enough room to do it this way you're left with two choices.

You can slide one foot to the side and then slide the other after it, such that they both fit on to the hold. If the foothold is really small and there's not enough room for your other foot until the first one is off, the sliding technique could still work if you're precise enough that your foot slides on to the hold just as the first one slides off.

The alternative is somewhat more risky, but with good coordination it's very effective. It involves doing a small 'jump' with your foot, switching feet while in the air and then landing on the other foot. 'Jump' might be too strong of a word as you're not trying to jump high into the air, but just high enough for you to sneak one foot underneath the other. We're only talking a few centimetres here. You'll also be able to slow the speed of your jump if the handholds allow it.

We suggest you practise matching feet down low on the bouldering wall, as here you'll usually find lots of good holds. Try traversing the whole wall and match your feet on all the footholds you use. Vary the wall angle and size of the footholds. Use poorer and poorer handholds, so that you can't just 'cheat' by pulling up with your arms.

 Train all forms of foot matching – it will definitely come in handy!

STRONG FEET

Keeping your feet on the wall when it's steep is very challenging. It requires a combination of strength and technique. The best exercise for targeting this skill is to climb steep walls while focusing on keeping your feet on the wall as you're moving up. You should stand on your toes and avoid using heel and toe hooks. Maintain tension throughout your body – from your hands to your feet. Chances are you'll fall the second you release the tension. It's important to start with good footholds and shorter moves and then progressively up the difficulty by increasing the distance between the holds and by using smaller footholds. The exercise becomes significantly harder when the movements speed up, so start by doing static moves only, and then gradually make your moves more dynamic.

> Use aggressive shoes with a downturned toe box. They will allow you to maintain pressure on the footholds when the wall is steep. Think of your toes as hooks that grip behind the edges of the holds. On small footholds, there might not be any edge to catch, but we've found that it helps to keep the same focus.

TRICKSTER

The opposite of the previous exercise, now it's time to climb steep routes or boulder problems using all the tricks of the trade so as not to cut loose with your feet. Toe and heel hooks make it significantly easier to keep your feet on the wall when things get steep, as in many cases they remove the need for maintaining tension throughout your body.

Start with shorter moves and climb statically. Gradually increase the lengths of the moves, making them more dynamic. Walls ranging from 40 degrees overhanging to full-on roofs are great for this exercise.

 You can 'bicycle' (i.e. stand on top of a hold while toe hooking on the same hold) on almost any hold when it's steep. Even tiny foot chips can be used for toe hooking to take some of the load off in overhangs.

GRIP POSITIONS

IT'S IMPORTANT TO be able to use different grip positions when we're climbing. In *The Climbing Bible* we defined open hand, pinch, half crimp and crimp. We pointed out that the more aggressive grip positions, like the half crimp and crimp, allow for larger and more explosive movements, while the open-handed grip lends itself to a more precise and careful style of climbing. In addition, a hold will often dictate the best way of holding it. To be versatile climbers we must train the different grip positions, and the following pages demonstrate some exercises for doing just that.

PHOTO: THILO SCHRÖTER
Martin Mobråten pinching hard with his left hand in order to send *Eye of Sauron* (Font 7c+), Rocklands, South Africa.

GRIP POSITIONS

Open hand

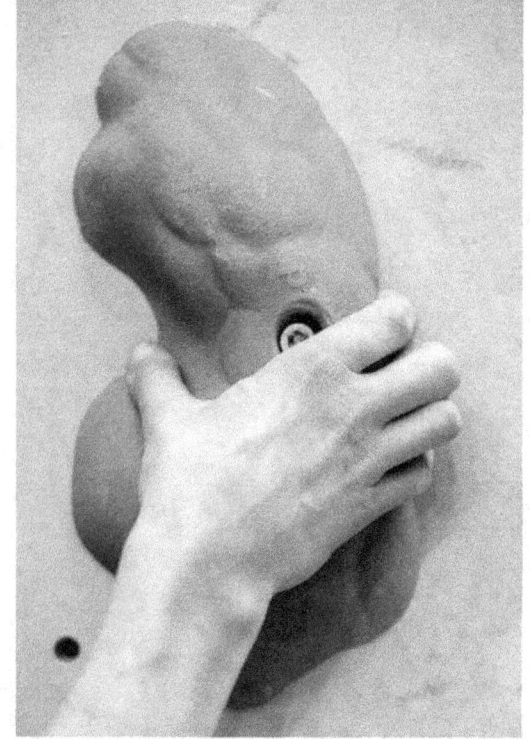

Pinch

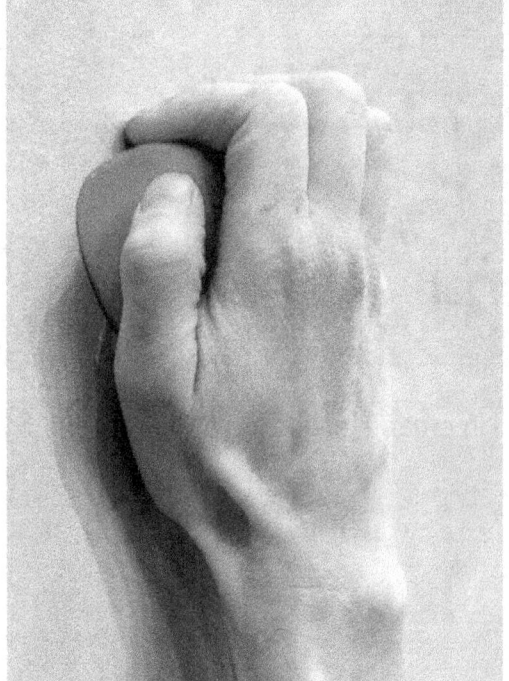

Half crimp

Crimp

LET THE HOLD DECIDE

Most of us have a go-to grip position we prefer and resort to when we get pumped; by doing this we'll get stronger at using our preferred grip position, but we also need to get stronger in the other positions as well. To practise this, climb a route or boulder problem you've sent before. Use an open-handed grip on all the pockets and good holds, use a half crimp on all edges, and pinch every pinchable hold. Be strict, and ask a climbing buddy to be a judge and let you know if you're cheating.

PRACTISING YOUR CRIMPS

In our experience, many climbers struggle with the half crimp and crimp when starting their climbing careers. The most common grip position for beginners is the open-handed grip. This is a good thing, as this grip minimises the risk of injuries, but it also limits your climbing. By simply standing on the ground while training the half crimp and crimp on an edge, you have a safe and easy method of getting comfortable with the grip positions before putting them to good use on the wall. When you have placed the grip properly, you can bend your knees slightly and start to load the grip – just enough to give you an idea of how it will feel to use the grip while climbing. Hanging from the edge can be trained specifically through deadhangs and is described further in chapter 2.

Be careful with the crimp. This grip is an important weapon when needed, but it should not be used too much during training.

BALANCE

GOOD BALANCE ON the wall is perhaps the most important skill to master in order to conserve energy while climbing. Just think how much extra power you need to cling on to the wall when you lose balance, or how taxing it is to climb routes where you're constantly pushed off balance – like when you're laybacking. In *The Climbing Bible* we defined being in balance as having your centre of gravity centred on your area of support. In simple terms this means having your hips balanced between your feet. Wide foot placements make it easier to maintain balance. It's the same principle as when standing on the ground; if you're standing with wide feet you won't tip over if your buddy gives you a nudge, but with your feet together it's easy to lose balance and fall. Here are some good exercises to train your balance on the wall.

Balance is best trained on slabs and vertical or slightly overhanging walls. Use poor handholds, preferably slopers.

PHOTO: BJØRNAR SMESTAD
Stian Christophersen sending *Direkterekyl* (F8b+), Bergflødt, Norway. The combination of small handholds and footholds, where most of them are either sidepulls or gastons, makes this route a proper testpiece for balance and weight distribution.

WEIGHT DISTRIBUTION

Pull on with two not-too-good handholds on the wall, and use two footholds which are spaced slightly further apart than the handholds. Move your right hand to a hold further up to the right and back down again, then move your left hand to a hold up to the left and back again. Before moving your hand, move your body from side to side to find the position with the best balance. Start with larger movements and gradually make them smaller as you start to find the balance point.

Get your body used to finding a sense of balance. This is an important skill you'll need throughout your climbing career. Even experienced climbers depend on this every time they're facing challenging and technical moves on small holds. It might look like they're 'just' climbing, but even they are forced to use their body to get a feel for what's right for them.

TRAVERSING

Traversing is a simple yet effective exercise for training balance. When moving sideways, you're forced to constantly shift your centre of gravity to maintain balance. Mainly using sidepulls will add to the need for finding the right body positions. Add in a bit of traversing as a part of every warm-up, and focus on climbing in control and in balance.

 Choose walls with lots of holds, which will allow you to use larger footholds and smaller handholds.

LOCKING OFF
If you are forced to lock off in order to grip a tiny hold where you really have to place every digit perfectly on to vanishingly small features, you

will be dependent on finding the perfect balance so as not to miss the hold or waste energy. The same goes for clipping the draws when climbing on lead. A good exercise for training balance is therefore to climb easy routes but lock off for 1 to 3 seconds each time before grabbing the next hold. Here it's important that you find the optimal balance before you move your hand to the next hold. To make the exercise more difficult you can climb progressively harder routes.

 Climb on vertical routes and take your time!

MATCHING

If you have to match a hold, you're dependent on finding the right body position such that you're in balance when matching – especially if the hold you're matching is a sloper. You'll also have to lower your body, in order to get a better angle in relation to the hold. For this exercise you should climb routes well within your limit and match every possible hold as you climb. When you've climbed several routes by matching all the holds you can play with harder routes and find which holds feel natural to match. It's often advantageous to match holds if you're about to do a long move and if the hold is large enough to fit both your hands. It can also be smart to match hands before a high foot placement, but climbing is a sport with many exceptions, so you'll have to get a feel for it yourself.

NO MATCHING
'No matching' is well known in the climbing wall, but does this kind of training make us forget to match when we're supposed to perform? Regardless of the answer, it's important to also train matching to become familiar with the advantages it can yield on the wall.

FIND THE REST
Finding good resting positions on a route is an excellent way to train your balance. In order to be able to rest you have to lower your body, get as much weight on to your feet as possible and, most important, find your balance. If you're not in balance you will have to use unnecessary amounts

of energy to stay in place and you won't be able to rest properly. We suggest trying to climb vertical routes two to three grades below your maximum, and trying to find five rests where you can hang for 20 to 30 seconds. It's important that you can breathe calmly, shake your hands and chalk up if you need to.

 If you can comfortably hang with a straight arm on an open-handed grip, you've probably found a good resting position.

PHOTO: MARTIN MOBRÅTEN

Outdoor routes are often comprised of hard sequences followed by good rests. Learning how to rest while climbing is therefore an important skill to master if you want to climb outside. Here, Arne Farestveit is relaxing before the crux of *The Eye of Odin* (F8c+), Flatanger, Norway.

CLIMBING WITHOUT PINCHING

It's better to avoid pinching when training balance. We sometimes call pinching the 'technique killer', because in many cases it removes the need for proper technique, as long as you're strong enough to pinch a hold. Pinching enables you to lean your body out from the wall and use your arms and hands to pull yourself in. This allows you to climb without having your body in the right position. Let's use a pinchable sidepull as an example:

If you pinch the hold you'll be able to lean out from the wall. If, on the other hand, you're only gripping the hold using an open hand you're forced to position your body to the side and in towards the wall in order to hang on.

Start by trying boulder problems or routes you know well and try to repeat them without pinching. Then you can move on to trying new routes in the same fashion.

CLIMBING WITH FEWER FINGERS

By adding limitations to how you grip the holds you'll automatically transfer more weight on to your feet. A hold which feels good can lead to you pulling too hard with your arms and being careless with the little details that decide whether or not you're in balance. By using only two or three fingers on each hold you'll reduce the chances of making these mistakes. You should perform this exercise on slabs or vertical walls so as not to put too much load on your fingers.

 Try a boulder problem using your preferred grip position. Then try climbing it with only three fingers on each hold, and then just two fingers. How does this affect your climbing?

ONE HAND ONLY
To make things even more challenging, try climbing a few boulder problems using only one hand. For this exercise it's important that you choose vertical walls or slabs, and problems with relatively large footholds. By taking the time to find your balance before moving your

hand to the next hold you can maintain full control while climbing.

> Find your balance, trust your feet and do short moves.

NO HANDS

As a final challenge, try to climb without using any hands at all. You'll need to find boulder problems on slabs with large holds or volumes for standing on. Start by using all available footholds before progressing to single problems. Make smaller steps to avoid losing your balance.

 To make sure this is a balance exercise, try to move as calmly as possible to maintain balance throughout the movement. If it's not possible to do a certain move statically and in control, try to generate as little speed as you can.

PHOTO: KNUT LERHOL
Martin Mobråten trying to climb without using his hands.

JOHNNY'S METHOD

British climber Johnny Dawes is well known for his impeccable technique and, at that time, unconventional training methods. He used to combine slabs and dynamics in ways that were almost unheard of. Outdoors, and especially on slabs, you were supposed to climb in a controlled way and not move dynamically between often poor holds. About 20 years ago Johnny was holding a climbing clinic at the Tyrili Climbing Centre in Oslo. We took part in this clinic and to be quite honest, we didn't think it was any good. We were mostly instructed to climb with our hands on our backs, and only on the really difficult problems were we allowed to perhaps use just one finger. Come on! We wanted to climb hard and we realised this was never going to make us any stronger. We left the clinic disappointed, without feeling neither better nor smarter. But here we are, 20 years later, and we've written a book filled with exercises that are eerily similar to what Johnny tried to teach us. Johnny believed you had to challenge your familiar repertoire of movements, limit the way you could do moves and try new things all the time. After a couple of decades we've come to realise the same thing. Not all the time of course; there's much to be gained from training basic skills and we should be training 'regular' climbing as well, but that's basically what we do on the wall all the time anyway. That's why it's so important to challenge ourselves with new exercises and new variants of moves we've done before. We hope this story and this book inspires you to try something new.

TENSION & DIRECTION OF FORCE

IN ORDER TO achieve tension and the correct direction of force you need to position yourself in such a way that you can use the holds in the best way possible. This is essential when climbing on sidepulls and undercuts. Just imagine how difficult it is to use a right-hand sidepull if there's no foothold further out to the right that allows you to weight the sidepull. Similarly, you can use opposite-facing surfaces to create tension between the holds. For example, imagine climbing a prow with slopers on both sides. The holds by themselves might be terrible, but because you can compress between them they might even feel rather good.

The exercises to train tension and direction of force resemble the exercises for training balance, but they are mostly performed on steeper walls. The central point here is mostly about positioning in relation to the holds and in which direction to push or pull, and not solely about making fine adjustments to your centre of gravity. The following pages feature suggested exercises.

PHOTO: ENDRE VIK

Maria Davies Sandbu tensioning up on *Wolverine* (Font 8b+), Vingsand, Norway.

FINDING THE POSITION
To train yourself to get into the correct position to execute moves, try climbing routes where you have full control of every move. Don't take shortcuts by moving dynamically or kipping past tricky sections.* You should position yourself in such a way that you can do every move

statically, or close to it.

*   'Kipping' means to swing dynamically through a move, either because of necessity or the inability to do the move in a controlled fashion.

SIDEPULLS ONLY

For this exercise, as far as it's possible, try to climb only on sidepulls. You should choose a wall with lots of holds so that you have a good selection of sidepulls when climbing. Don't worry about the colour of the holds or the intentions of the route setters. Focus on finding the right body position for every move to stay in control when moving up the wall. It's important to climb on relatively easy routes so that you have enough strength to complete the exercise in good style.

 When you have completed this exercise a few times, try doing it without pinching the holds. This will require even better body positioning.

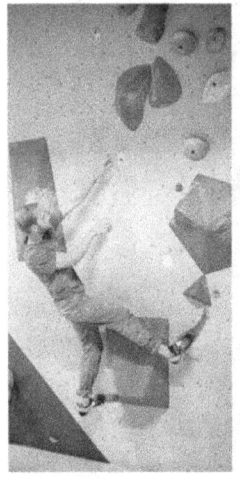    

CROSSING THE LINE

For this exercise, start on two good handholds on the bouldering wall. The wall should be vertical or slightly overhanging, and you can use any footholds. Now cross your left hand past your centre line, so that both of your hands are on the same side of your centre line. After completing the cross move, position your body so that you're ready to release your right hand and move it to a hold that's further to the right. Repeat the exercise with your right hand. Now you can play around and see how far you can do each cross move. As the cross moves start to get longer, it'll become natural for you to turn your left hip into the wall when crossing with your left hand, and vice versa.

 Try crossing from a sidepull to a sidepull that faces in the opposite direction. How does this affect your body position as you prepare to do the next move?

THE ADVANTAGES OF TWISTING: MARTIN SHARES A STORY

I started climbing over 20 years ago at Møt Veggen ['Meet the Wall', Ed.], a climbing wall in Skøyen, Oslo. There was a climber there named Markus. Markus wasn't particularly muscular nor was he very strong, but he moved like a cat on the wall. I found this fascinating and I would just sit and observe Markus climbing. What I noticed was that he twisted in on a lot of the moves. By using this technique he was able to climb hard grades without using a lot of strength. This was something I had to try. For a while, I was trying to twist in on every move. After some time I realised that this wasn't always helping, but I had still learned a technique that quite often proved itself useful. Using this technique removed a lot of the need for power when just fronting hard moves, and I was able to do the moves more easily as I positioned myself from side to side by twisting in.

COMPRESSION

To train compression we want you to climb prows and test out different body positions. Use any holds for hands and feet, and try to find a prow with a lot of holds for this exercise, so that you have many options to choose between. Try climbing the prow with a 'T-rex' compression, a wide compression and a nearly fully stretched-out compression.† Start with footholds that place you in a position with your arms at shoulder height, then try using footholds that are slightly too low and then slightly too high, because then you'll have to compress with your arms either above or below your shoulders.

How strong you are at compressing in different positions can vary greatly. As a general rule, you're strongest when your hands are placed relatively wide and at shoulder height. It's also advantageous if your right and left hands are placed at equal distances from your right and left shoulders, respectively. In other words, you should strive for symmetry and not offset positions when compressing.‡

---

† We call it T-rex compression when both handholds are near one another. The closer they are to your centre line, the more your arms will look like those of a Tyrannosaurus rex. This position offers less than ideal working conditions for the muscles in your chest, meaning you'll be weaker in this position than if the handholds were placed further apart and you were compressing wider.

‡ Offset means that the holds are at different heights in relation to one another.

T-REX
You're not strong in the T-rex position, so try to avoid it if you can.

PHOTO: MARTIN MOBRÅTEN
Maria Davies Sandbu compressing between the holds to send *More than I Had* (Font 8a), Flatanger, Norway.

DYNAMICS

MOVING DYNAMICALLY IS both a technical and mental challenge. Technically, you want to lower your body so that most of the movement is generated by the larger muscles in your legs, and then use your arms to guide your momentum towards the next hold. As you reach the next hold with your hand you'll want your body close to the wall and at the apex of its upward trajectory – the point where your body stops to move before it begins to fall back down again. In order to achieve this, you will need to allow your body to move away from the wall slightly at the start of the movement, and then pull it in towards the wall as you move up. You also need to have the correct timing, so that you have just enough speed to reach the next hold with your body in the position you want. For many, it's a mental challenge to let go and move fast for the next hold. This mental barrier will hinder your progression as a climber, because the benefits of moving dynamically are great. You can do bigger and harder moves, and you'll save energy by swinging between the holds instead of locking off.

In our experience, it's best to start training dynamic climbing by doing exercises that don't require lots of speed and coordination. As long as the walls aren't too steep you should be able to perform the moves quite slowly and you'll have plenty of time before you have to grab the next hold. This will allow you to focus on the technical execution and build confidence on these types of moves. By starting easy you'll start to believe that these moves are possible – even for you.

DYNAMIC MOVES
A dynamic move is not the same as a dyno. Using speed to reach the next hold is not the same as jumping for it.

PHOTO: MARTIN MOBRÅTEN
Stian Christophersen swinging his way up *Diamanten* (Font 8b), Vingsand, Norway.

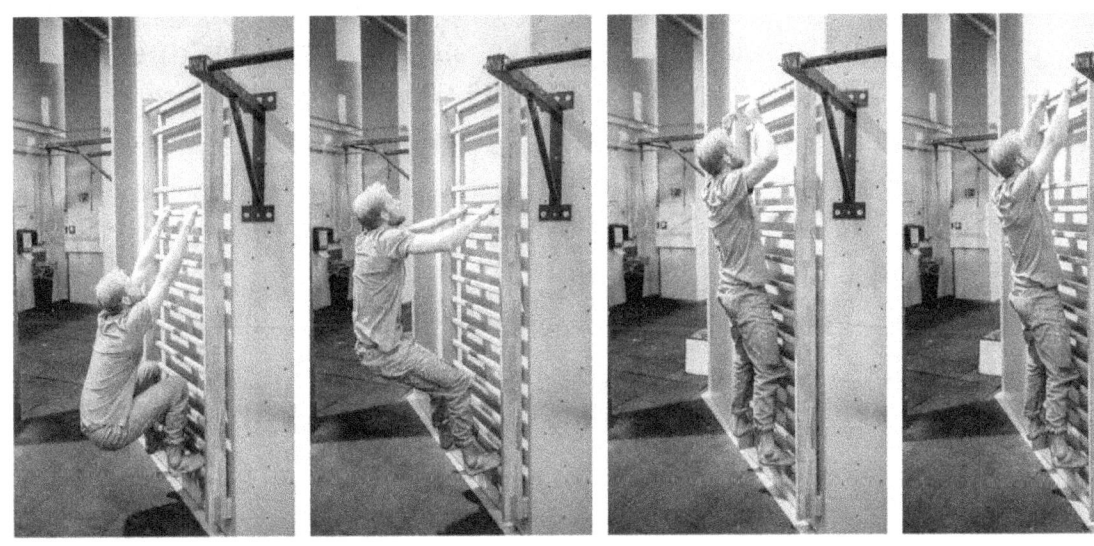

WALL BARS

Wall bars are a great place to start your dynamic training. You can easily find the level that's right for you, and focus on correct technical execution and gain confidence in doing dynamic moves. Here's a progression ladder you can use:

- Start by holding the same bar with both hands and stand on a bar that has you bending your knees at 90 degrees or more when your arms are straight. Push with your legs and shoot upwards, while at the same time pulling yourself in towards the wall with your arms. Move one arm up to the highest bar you can reach. Grab the bar with a slight bend in the elbow. Switch arms and repeat. To make the exercise harder you can place your feet higher, but still start with your hands on the same bar as before. This requires more strength in your arms to pull your body in towards the wall – the movement will be faster, and it will be harder to get the right timing. Continue repeating the exercise with both hands until you get the timing right, meaning you are grabbing the top bar with your hips against the wall and your body at the apex of its upward movement.

- Repeat the exercise, but this time move both hands to the highest bar you can reach. This is more challenging mentally, as you have to let go of the bars completely, but as long as your feet aren't too high, you'll notice that you actually have quite a bit of time. If you think it's too scary you can start by going for the next bar above your starting bar, and then increase the distance. As you get more comfortable with the exercise, try clapping your hands before grabbing the next bar. With a bit of practice, you'll notice you can clap one, two or even three times before grabbing the next bar. As with the previous exercise, repeat this exercise over and over until your timing is perfect.
- To make this exercise even harder still, try also moving sideways in addition to upwards. This time you should grab the next bar either to the right or the left of your starting position. You'll have to lower your body to generate speed upwards, but also swing from side to side to create the correct arch towards the bar. This requires even better timing, but is also more relevant to climbing. Again, repeat the exercise until your timing is perfect.

 If you don't have access to wall bars you can also do this exercise on a vertical wall with a good selection of jugs, so that you can easily adjust the difficulty.

DOWN AND UP

For this exercise, choose a route you know well. The wall should be slightly overhanging and the holds should be quite good. Lower your body and start every move with your arms straight. Initiate the upward movement with your legs and pull your body towards the wall with your arms. Try to deadpoint the moves and grab the next hold with your elbow slightly bent, so that you're able to lock off your body as you stick the hold.

 Try to flow through the movement and avoid unnatural changes in direction or stopping after the movement has been initiated.

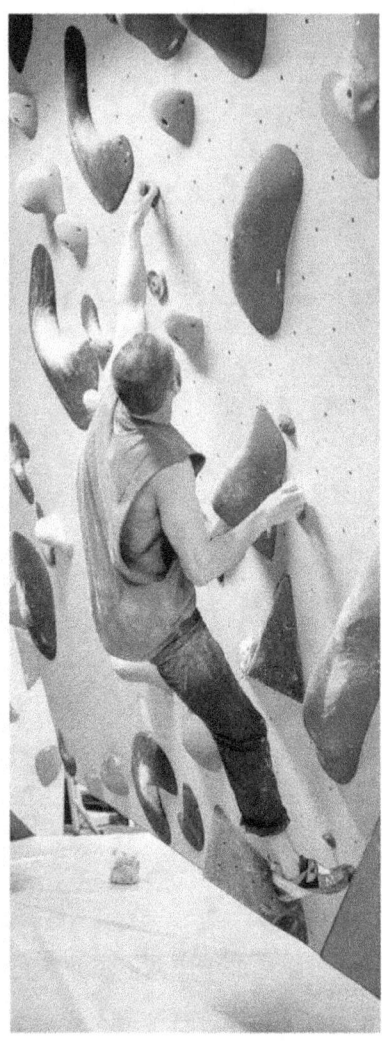

DEADLY PRECISION

Choose two good holds on a vertical or slightly overhanging wall and choose footholds at a comfortable height. The goal here is to move dynamically to a hold that's higher up than you are able to reach statically, but not higher than you're able to reach after trying a few times. When you feel you're in control of the move, repeat it at least 10 more times. Even if you can do the move first go, it's far from certain that you're executing it perfectly, and the goal of this exercise is to perfect the movement. A good indicator of how well you're executing the move is how much energy you're spending to stop the movement as you grab the hold you're going for. In theory, you shouldn't be using any more force to stick the hold than if you were to do the move statically, but this won't be the case if your hips are too far away from the wall and your body is still in motion. Therefore, you need to actively work on these key elements on every try. Think about how the move feels, video yourself and get feedback from others. When you feel you have optimised the move, switch hands and repeat the exercise.

Cecilie using a sloper and a guide hold.

To make the exercise harder, you can add rules for how you're allowed to grip the holds. It'll be significantly harder if you're only allowed to grab even relatively good holds with just three or two fingers. Don't try to grab holds with just two fingers before you've practised the move, as too much force on your fingers as you stick the move can lead to strained muscles in your forearm. The next step is to choose holds that require a bit more aim, for example pockets, blocked holds or slopers. These will require a higher degree of precision in your movement. Repeat the different variants 10 times each and search for the perfect execution. As a last challenge we want you to make the starting holds worse.

Here are some suggestions for challenging starting positions:

- Small, positive holds allow you to drop your hips away from the wall slightly to create speed in towards the wall as you reach the next hold. It's likely that you will have to start moving in towards the wall sooner than if you were starting on jugs. It will be harder for your fingers and it will require a higher degree of precision in your movement.
- Use a sloper with your upper hand and a better hold – a guide hold – for your lower hand. A positive sidepull or an undercut is preferable for your lower hand, so that you can compress between the holds. This will allow you to drop your hips away from the wall a bit to create momentum in the right direction in order to reach the next hold with the correct body position. You should be grabbing the next hold with your lower hand from the guide hold, and not the hand which is on the sloper.
- Using two opposing slopers is even more challenging, but if you can compress between them you can create the right momentum towards the next hold.

REPETITION
If you find it boring to repeat the same move 10 times, consider the fact that the Japanese competition climbers, arguably the best team in the world at the moment, often play around on the same move for up to an hour before moving on to the next part of their programme.

DYNOS

We don't want to give too many pointers for your dyno training. Simply put, you should be playing around with as many different dynos as possible. Start with simple dynos between good holds on vertical walls. Do both regular and double dynos, so dyno with just one hand or both hands, and gradually increase the lengths of the dynos and the steepness of the wall as you gain confidence with these moves. It's usually advantageous to overdo the speed a bit, so that you land with your elbows bent. This way you'll be able to quickly pull up to avoid an unnecessarily large swing. Focus on locking off your body as much as possible as you stick the hold.

 Always incorporate double dynos at the end of your specific warm-up routine. This activates the muscles and helps you to loosen up mentally.

ARCHING

Doing a sideways arch instead of moving straight up towards the next hold can be especially advantageous when climbing on sidepulls. To train these types of moves, find a layback edge or use the side of a large volume. Grab the edge with one hand and find a hold lower down with your other hand, as with the exercise with the sloper and the guide hold mentioned earlier. The footholds should be relatively high, so that you're able to do a long move to the next handhold. Now, if you try to move straight up to the next hold, your centre of gravity won't be far enough to the side and the direction of force will be all wrong. You will therefore have to start the movement by shifting your centre of gravity to the side and away from the sidepull, before pushing up with your legs to create upward momentum.

CROSS MOVES
When doing dynamic cross moves where you cut your feet from the wall,

you should open your hips and front the wall instead of twisting in. This is especially relevant when the wall is overhanging. If twisting in, your body would continue to rotate after completing the movement, which might make it difficult to hold the swing. If you front the wall instead you'll avoid this rotation, because your body's initial relative position is the same as when you land the next hold.

To begin with we recommend that you stand on the ground below a steep wall (preferably 40 to 60 degrees overhanging) and try to jump to a hold with one hand while holding a handhold lower down with the other. It should be a cross move, so if you are to jump with your right hand, the hold you are aiming for should be further to the left than the hold you are jumping from. First, try to jump while facing towards the hold you're jumping to, then turn and jump while facing the wall.

Vary the length of the cross move and notice the effect it has on your rotation and how you should position yourself before you jump. If you really overdo it, you might have to start with your back against the hold you're jumping to (see photos). It will feel like you're jumping backwards, but even though this might feel wrong, it's still correct.

The next step is to do this on the wall. As long as the holds are good enough you can use the same holds as before. And as before, start by twisting your hips in and position yourself as if you were to do the move statically, but try to jump to the hold. Then choose footholds that force you to open your hips and front the wall – there's no twisting in this time. Vary the length of the cross move and see what happens.

TRICKS

MODERN PROBLEMS REQUIRE modern solutions which you'll need to master if you want to climb hard problems indoors or participate in bouldering competitions. Techniques and styles like 'flicking', 'clutch' and 'wall runs' are commonplace and require a great deal of coordination. You should therefore regularly practise these techniques in order to master them.

Luckily, they usually look the same on the wall, with the holds arranged in the same way, so you can practise these techniques without the boulder problem being set in this exact way.

It's easy to forget the fundamental elements when practising more advanced moves. Therefore, always remember that dynamic moves should start away from and move in towards the wall, and that the movement should be as close to a deadpoint as possible. Also remember which compression position you're the strongest in, as flicks and clutch moves require compression strength.

PHOTO: BJØRN HELGE RØNNING
Stian Christophersen on the last problem in the final of the 2017 Norwegian National Bouldering Championships. At the start of the boulder problem you had to do a dyno while at the same time flicking your right foot into a toe hook. From there you had to do a double clutch out of this position to top the problem.

 Focus on the first hold you're going for and let your other hand find the other hold naturally.

FLICK

A flick is when you move one hand to a hold and, either in the same movement or immediately after, have to turn – flick – the other hand to another hold in order to maintain your position. The hold arrangement is usually similar to what is shown in the photo, with sidepulls all facing the same way and the hold you're flicking to facing the other way. Start by practising on vertical walls with very good holds and short moves, where you don't really have to flick at all: the idea is to practise the technique and get used to it on easier climbs. After mastering the technique on good holds, you can progress to smaller and more slopey holds, and then increase the distance between them and choose steeper walls.

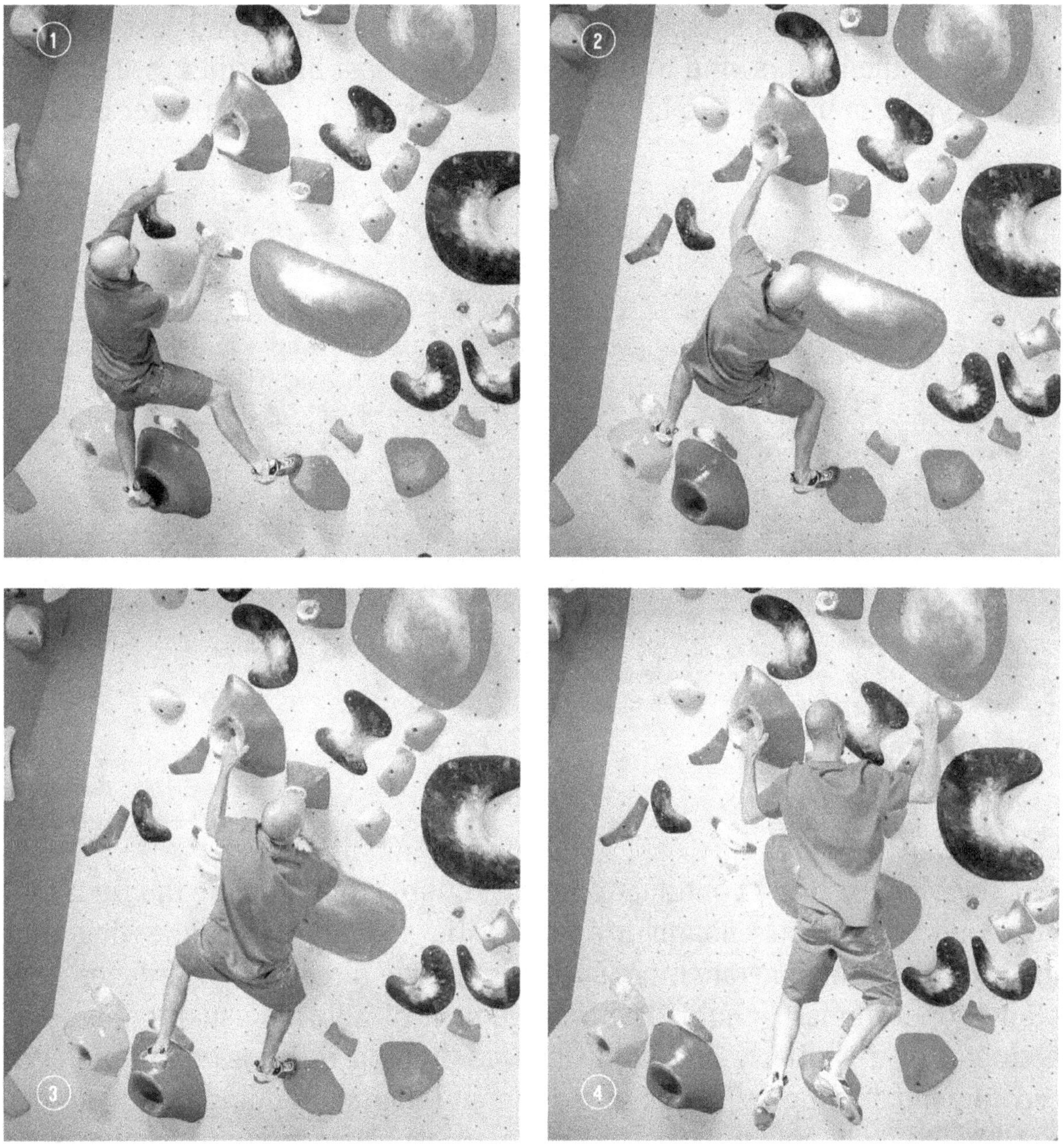

 Look at the first hold you're going for and let your other hand swing naturally to the other hold.

CROSS CLUTCH

A cross clutch is when you're do a cross move and just as you grab the first hold you continue with your other hand to the next hold in order to achieve a better position. The hold arrangement is almost always a cross to a sidepull and then paddling to another but opposing sidepull. Start practising on slightly overhanging walls and good holds that are ever-so-slightly positioned as sidepulls. Do a short cross move, and just as your hand lands the hold, swing to the next hold that's a bit further away. After a while you can progress to bigger moves, steeper walls and poorer holds.

DOUBLE CLUTCH

The double clutch is a continuation of the double dyno, where the first hold you land isn't good enough for you to be able to hold the swing, but instead is used to generate more speed or change direction towards the next – and hopefully last – hold. The arrangement of holds is usually a dyno to a sloper, or a similarly bad hold, then continuing on to a good hold. We recommend starting by dynoing to a jug and then continuing on to another jug immediately above. After a while you can play around by increasing the distance between the holds, adding sideways movements and using poorer holds. We recommend doing this exercise on walls that are around 20 to 40 degrees overhanging.

How much of the swing you should try to control on the first hold before moving on to the next can vary a lot. Generally, it's better to move quickly if the first hold is bad and the next hold is good. If, on the other hand, the first hold is good, it's better to try to stop the swing as much as possible before moving on to the next hold. We recommend that you play around so you that you get a feel for what's best.

INDUSTRY OF COOL

There's a boulder problem in Rocklands, South Africa, called *Industry of Cool*. The crux of this boulder is a double dyno around a steep prow to a sloper that's so bad you need to make a clutch move with your right hand into a good hold in a crack. Because it's hard to hold the swing on the sloper, it's natural to pull up and move on to the next hold quite quickly, which is exactly what Thilo Schröter and I (Martin), were attempting, again and again, some time in 2017. We felt we were really close, but we were never able to stick the good hold in the crack. I'm pretty sure I've tried that move over a hundred times spread out over several days and trips to the area. And always with the same result: I'm unable to hold the swing long enough to reach the next good hold. After watching a video of American climber Dave Graham sending the problem, we returned a few days later with a new tactic. In the video, Dave takes most of the swing with his arms straight before, at the end of the swing, he elegantly and frighteningly easily pulls into the crack. After just a few attempts, Thilo managed to stick the move and quickly found himself on top of the boulder. It still wasn't easy, but the new tactic worked. This just shows that the theory of pulling up early on bad holds isn't always correct. Sometimes it's about muscle power and pulling up, other times it's about 'skeleton style' and straight arms.

PHOTO: MIKE MULLINS

Bjørn Sætnan on *Industry of Cool* (Font 8a+). Bjørn is taller than most and found his own way of sticking the sloper – by not letting go of the starting hold. This is one of the things that's so cool about climbing – you can find your own way up, using the resources you have. It's still really hard the way Bjørn climbed it, but his post on Instagram was hashtagged

#cruxesareforshortpeople ...

 Try standing far out on the starting volume as this makes it easier to generate momentum in towards the wall.

WALL RUNS

Wall runs are a popular addition to competition climbing because they make for spectacular viewing. They entail running/jumping on holds, usually volumes, without any handholds to grab on to along the way. To start practising wall runs all you need is a few volumes low to the ground and a selection of good handholds. Close-to-vertical walls are best, but slabs and slightly overhanging walls will do just fine too. To begin with, play around with short moves where there's no real need to run at all.

Maybe all you need is a step to the side in order to reach the next hold. Then you can progress by increasing the distances between the holds – this will require more speed and better coordination. Also play around with sidepulls and poorer holds.

THINK OUTSIDE THE BOX
Before the 2018 Norwegian Bouldering Championships in Trondheim, several of the local athletes paid multiple visits to Rush Trampoline Park in order to improve their dynamic abilities from a technical and mental standpoint. Just think about it – a small deadpoint move on the wall will be less challenging if you did a backflip on the trampoline the day before.

COMBINATION EXERCISES

CLIMBING IS TECHNICALLY complex, and you constantly have to solve new problems while climbing. You have to deal with delicate footwork while at the same time trying to maintain balance, in addition to having to choose between using speed or locking off for the next move. The exercises we have presented so far more or less focus on isolated elements, and it's important to be able to master each element separately. But while climbing it's also important to keep all of these elements in your mind so you are quickly able to choose the most appropriate technique for the situation and to combine the different elements, if necessary. Here's a selection of exercises to help you practise this.

PHOTO: HENNING WANG
Maria Davies Sandbu fighting her way up the last rail on *Nordic Plumber* (F8c), Flatanger, Norway.

STATIC VS DYNAMIC

Part of what makes climbing difficult is figuring out how to attack a move. Should you take your time – finding the perfect balance – and execute the move statically and in full control, or should you swing through the move and do it dynamically? A good exercise for practising these choices is to climb a selection of boulder problems by first doing all the moves statically, and then doing them dynamically. After completing all of the problems twice, try to combine the moves in the best way possible. Which moves were easier to do statically, and which moves were easier to do dynamically? Be honest with yourself. If you're a static climber you have to be conscious of this and not think that all the moves were easier to do statically. If you find this difficult, you can discuss it with a friend who has different qualities as a climber to yourself. We would argue that it's always good to climb with people who have other strengths than yourself, so that you can learn the best parts of their climbing style and add these to your own.

 Start with easy boulder problems on slabs and vertical walls, to make sure you'll be able to do all of the moves statically.

5 PROBLEMS IN 5 MINUTES

To become better at adapting to different styles you should change between different wall angles and holds when climbing. A good exercise for training this skill is to climb five different boulder problems within 5 minutes. Choose one problem for each wall angle: slab, vertical, slightly overhanging, roughly 45-degree overhanging and roof. It's good if these are problems you've tried before so that you know what to do and you know you'll be able to climb them. Climb all of them one after the other, with just a short break in between each problem. It's important that you focus on climbing them as perfectly as you can, adapting your style to match that of the problem. It's highly likely that precision footwork and balance will be key for the less-steep walls, while dynamics and direction of force will be important for the steeper climbs.

Marius Moe (2 metres tall) copying Sunniva Øvre Eide (1.69 metres).

COPYCAT

We all have our preferred climbing style, and in many instances it's either going to be the controlled, static style, or the more loose, dynamic style. A good exercise to challenge your familiar movement pattern is to climb a boulder problem in exactly the same way as your climbing partner. The bigger the difference between you and your partner, the more challenging the exercise will be. Ideally you will be at roughly the same level, but it's advantageous if your partner has differing strengths to you.

If you're a static climber, you'll learn a lot from copying a more dynamic climber. And in the same way, a tall climber can learn a lot by copying a short climber, as they'll then be challenged by compressed positions and high feet.

PROBLEM-SOLVING
When climbing, you're constantly having to solve problems: how to place your feet, how to grip the holds, whether you should move dynamically, whether you should twist in or front the wall. To become better at solving these problems, which are often split-second decisions, here's a good

exercise. Pick five new boulder problems that have recently been set at your climbing wall and try to climb them all within 20 minutes. You should probably bring a stopwatch to keep track of time. You have an average of 4 minutes per problem and these minutes disappear quickly.

 If there aren't any new problems at your wall, you can either visit a different wall or ask a friend to make up some problems for you.

TRAINING FOR TRAD & ALPINE

MARTINE LIMSTRAND is one of Norway's best trad and alpine climbers. She started out as a competition climber and has therefore logged countless hours of technique and strength training. We asked Martine to write a few words on how she feels these hours have helped her trad climbing.

Mastering climbing in alpine environments and placing your own gear is mostly about equipment and mental skills. Climbing past and falling on your own gear is difficult to practise without being outside, doing the work, placing the nuts and cams, and testing them. Still, there are many useful exercises you can do indoors to help you prepare. Generally speaking, improving your climbing skills will also make your mental game stronger, so by working on your footwork, finger strength and endurance, you can improve your trad climbing confidence.

Whether you wish to climb sustained cracks and corners, or you prefer varied multi-pitch climbing, having better endurance will always be an advantage. Alpine climbing often entails spending at least half an hour (or more) on a single pitch, and you're often gripping with the same hand for extended periods of time so you can place the right gear in the right spot. Even though you might not be able to practise placing gear indoors, it can be a good idea to do exercises indoors that improve your endurance and your ability to lock off.

Another element of alpine climbing is the long approaches. If you know you want to venture further into the outdoors, basic strength and endurance in your legs is important so that you have some strength and energy left over for the actual climbing. With proper technique you also use your legs and feet much more than your hands while climbing in alpine terrain. This you can practise indoors! Do exercises where you learn to trust bad footholds instead of pulling up with your arms. For example, try climbing slabs using just two or three fingers.

Remember: finger strength and slab climbing is more relevant than, for example, steep bouldering on big holds. Some climbing walls even have cracks that allow you to practise your jamming technique all through the winter months, which will come in handy!

PHOTO: OLA JAKOB DOVLAND
Martine enjoying herself at Fugløya, Norway.

CHAPTER 2

STRENGTH & POWER

PHOTO: THILO SCHRÖTER
Stian Christophersen on *Slashface* (Font 8b), Hueco Tanks, USA.

> Making every try count and taking enough time to rest is important. This second point in particular is often overlooked – even by us. Always ask yourself, 'Am I ready for another go now?' If the answer is yes, rest another minute or two, and then have a go with maximum effort.

BECOMING A STRONGER climber is a natural goal for most of us. Finger strength in relation to body weight is probably the most important physical factor for performance and one of the strongest indicators of what level we're climbing at. But gripping holds isn't the only thing we do on the wall. We also have to move between the holds, using the strength from our arms, upper body and what we can call our *core*.* In some cases, we need to move quickly, at other times as calmly as possible, and there's a difference between what is required of us physically when climbing on walls that are 60 degrees overhanging versus 15 degrees overhanging. In order to become a better and more complete climber we therefore have to work on improving multiple different factors, and the exercises in this chapter will guide you through methods of doing exactly that.

To begin with, we would like to clarify certain aspects within strength training. The number of repetitions is almost irrelevant, as training will make you stronger as long as you are tired after each set. This means you can vary the *dosage* of each exercise and adapt it to what the focus is of that particular training session.‡ How hard each repetition is, or how hard each individual move is, will influence how many repetitions or moves you'll be able to complete for each set, and here it's important to consider what you're actually training for. If your goal is to improve your maximum strength so you can do harder moves, boulder problems or crux sections on a route, it's more relevant to train at maximum effort with fewer repetitions. If your goal is to build a more general base so that you become stronger and can endure more training, it will be more relevant with a higher training *volume*.‡ Volume and effort must also be considered in relation to resting times. In general, the closer you are to maximum effort, the longer your rests should be. The dosage we have suggested for the following exercises is not set in stone, and should therefore be used only as a guide, based on what we feel will be more efficient in terms of becoming a stronger and better climber. As we stated in *The Climbing Bible*, training individualisation is an important principle, and this is also valid here.

Another important aspect to be aware of when it comes to strength training is the relationship between force and velocity. How much force a muscle can generate is dependent on how fast it has to contract, and with an increase in velocity there will be a decrease in the rate of force development. The ability to rapidly develop force is therefore different to developing force in static positions or during slower movements. We call this ability *power* or *explosive strength*, and we define it as the product *force x velocity*. Power is important in climbing, especially for boulderers, as they often have to create a lot of force quickly in order to perform a dynamic move. Additionally, the momentum has to be stopped when landing the next hold. With the value of power in climbing in mind, our training goal should be twofold: becoming stronger, and becoming faster. And for this reason, we have chosen to split the exercises in this chapter into strength and power. The primary difference between the two being the velocity at which the movements should be performed, but also how physically strenuous they are. Power is trained at maximum velocity in the movements and maximum effort in the landings and with less resistance or load than traditional strength training.

* *Core* is a term that normally describes the stomach and back. Us climbers could argue that the core is everything from the tips of our toes to the tips of our fingers, as we are dependent on maintaining a body position while moving an arm or a leg. However, for simplicity, we will still define the core as the musculature of the stomach and back.

† *Dosage* is the number of kg/intensity of each move x number of repetitions x number of sets per exercise.

‡ *Volume* is the number of repetitions x number of sets per exercise.

EXERCISES ON THE WALL

IN THIS PART we will cover exercises you can do on the climbing wall. By using the climbing wall as an arena for strength training you will include all the movement components that make up a climbing move. So, in addition to becoming stronger, you will also become better at moving and gain more from the training than if you were to only train strength through isolated exercises.

IMPORTANT CONSIDERATIONS FOR GETTING THE MOST OUT OF YOUR STRENGTH TRAINING

WHEN PLANNING TO train specific abilities during a session it's imperative that you're familiar with the training facilities. If your goal is to train finger strength on the bouldering wall, you either have to know which boulder problems are suitable for this, or you have to make up your own problems. Many climbing walls have their own training walls with a good selection of holds but without any pre-taped/set problems. This gives you the opportunity to make up problems that fit your exact needs for a session. Making up your own problems also has the added benefit of training your understanding of movements, so if your local wall has a section like this we highly recommend using it as much as possible.

> When you're making up boulder problems for sessions like this it's easier to choose equally sized holds that have an equal distance between them. If you can do one move with a slight margin, you can do four to six similar moves. To begin with you can use any footholds. As you get more proficient in making up problems, you can up the complexity by choosing specific footholds.

The most important aspects to consider if you're focusing on physical training when bouldering are grip type, the lengths of moves and wall angles. If your goal is finger strength, you should be climbing on small edges or pinches. If you're focusing on compression strength, you should climb on poorer holds that don't allow you to release tension between the holds. If you want to direct your training towards upper body and arm strength in order to be better at pulling through, the holds should be good enough for you to do the moves without matching.

As the walls get steeper, the more physically demanding it becomes for your fingers, arms and upper body, and you'll get less help from your legs. For less experienced climbers it can be challenging to train finger strength on walls steeper than 30 degrees, as the holds have to be relatively good just to be able to hang on. In this situation, walls steeper than 30 degrees can be used for training the arms, upper body and core, while less steep walls can be used for finger strength training as you then can allow yourself to use poorer holds. As you become stronger and more experienced, you'll be able to use poorer holds on steeper walls and hence increasingly be able to combine your training.

You can also use the size of the moves – the distance between the holds – as a variable. When doing short moves on bad holds, you can focus more on finger strength and tension between the fingers and toes, as the holds are too poor for you to cut your feet loose. Big moves on steep walls will require most of us to use relatively good holds independently of whether we're moving fast or slow between the holds, and the training will mostly target the arms, upper body and core rather than finger strength. Significantly increasing the distance between the holds is also a simple way to target power in your training.

To show how you can train specific elements on the bouldering wall, Stian will share some of his experiences from his own training:

MOVING SLOWLY WHEN YOU'RE GOOD AT MOVING FAST!

When I started climbing, I wasn't physically strong, neither in my fingers, nor in my arms or upper body. I was a rather petite little kid, something which isn't necessarily bad for climbing in general, but steep climbing and physically demanding positions definitely and literally weren't my strength. This wasn't something I reflected on too much when I was younger, and slowly but surely I developed a dynamic climbing style because this allowed me to solve harder moves by moving faster between holds. As I grew taller and stronger, I was able to do bigger moves on smaller holds. The dynamic style of climbing suited me well for bouldering and redpointing sport routes, but still I knew I had to become stronger. I had to become stronger in my fingers, stronger at moving slowly between holds and stronger at holding positions, so that I could lock off when the holds were too poor to do the moves while carrying a lot of speed.

So, one winter I decided to really focus on this, both through specific strength training and especially through my climbing. I made up steep boulder problems, removed any technical trickery like heel and toe hooks, and tried to climb with much less speed than what I normally would do. For example, I would try to lock off for a couple of seconds for every move, pulling slowly and steadily through a move without matching, or start the movement from down below and keep my feet on the wall throughout the problem. Over the course of the winter I noticed a gradual progression, but, rather worryingly, I also noticed I was doing worse on the not-so-steep climbing. Had I been training so much on my weaknesses that I had forgotten about my strengths? I couldn't find the natural flow and dynamic way of moving I was used to, and I noticed that I was making use of the slower movement pattern when I strictly didn't need to. When I realised this, I chose to create a more noticeable distinction in my training. I became more conscious of climbing dynamically and without restraining my technique for most of my climbing training, but I continued focusing on my weaknesses as a specific part of my training sessions.

I have on multiple occasions experienced that training our weaknesses can have a negative impact on our strengths, and albeit not as obvious as on this occasion it still emphasises the point – know thyself. Know your strengths and optimise them. Acknowledge what parts of your climbing you need to improve in order to progress, considering the physical, technical and mental factors. The trick is to maintain a balance between training your strengths and your weaknesses, and thereby develop your skills as a climber, step by step, for many years to come.

STRENGTH EXERCISES

MOUSE MOVES

The ability to hold on to small holds is one of the hallmarks of hard climbing and requires a great deal of finger strength. For this exercise you'll choose (or make up) one or more boulder problems on small holds with short moves. All the holds should be roughly the same size, all the moves roughly as hard, and you should be able to climb them with a controlled movement tempo. The focus should not be on pulling far or creating speed, but rather on using holds so small they barely enable you to hang on and move between them.

NUMBER OF MOVES PER PROBLEM: 6 to 8
REST: minimum 3 minutes
NUMBER OF TRIES IN TOTAL: 15 total, preferably 5 tries on 3 separate problems
WALL ANGLE: 15 to 60 degrees overhanging
HOLDS: small edges, pockets

 When you start training, we recommend using large, positive footholds.

THEMED BOULDERING

We're often stronger or weaker with different grip positions, and by making up problems with different themes we can choose to train specifically on both our strengths and our weaknesses. Make up problems consisting solely of pinches, edges, slopers or pockets. It can be a good idea to vary between different grip types throughout the session as this will increase both the technical and the physical benefits of the session and reduce the risk of injury caused by uniform training.

NUMBER OF MOVES PER PROBLEM: 5 to 6
REST: minimum 3 minutes
NUMBER OF TRIES IN TOTAL: 15 total, preferably 5 tries on 3 separate problems
WALL ANGLE: 15 to 60 degrees overhanging
HOLDS: small edges, pinches, pockets, slopers

4x4

This is a hard exercise where you'll have a lot of tries on relatively hard problems. In addition to becoming stronger, you'll also be improving your capacity so that you'll be able to climb longer boulder problems at your maximum level and be able to have more tries on your project per session. Choose four different problems, preferably with different grip types, movement patterns and wall angles. Climb problems one, two, three and four with a 60-second rest in between each problem. After problem four take a 3- to 5-minute rest and then repeat the whole process three more times so that in total you'll have 16 tries (four tries per problem). Since the resting time between each problem is short, the problems shouldn't be too close to your maximum level, so choose problems where you have enough of a margin so that you're able to rest enough between each try.

NUMBER OF MOVES PER PROBLEM: 6 to 8
REST: minimum 3 minutes
NUMBER OF TRIES IN TOTAL: 16 (4 tries on each problem on a circuit of 4 problems)
WALL ANGLE: vertical to roof, 1 problem per angle
HOLDS: varied

FEET ON THE WALL

We often see climbers falling because their feet cut loose on steep walls and they swing off. To avoid this, you need tension in your body from your fingers to your toes so that your feet remain stuck to the wall. This requires strength in your arms, upper body and core – we call this *body strength*. To train this specific body strength you should climb steep boulder problems where you're not allowed to cut loose. Start with good handholds and footholds to maintain control of the movements, and then use poorer handholds, and finally use poorer footholds.

NUMBER OF MOVES PER PROBLEM: 5 to 6
REST: minimum 3 minutes
NUMBER OF TRIES IN TOTAL: 15 total, preferably 5 tries on 3 separate problems
WALL ANGLE: 40 degrees and steeper
HOLDS: start with good holds, then make them as bad as possible as you progress

CAMPUSING

Footless climbing, or campusing, is a simple and fun way to train strength. For this exercise you'll be climbing problems without using your feet, which will obviously make it significantly harder for your fingers, arms and upper body.

If you've never done any campus training before, we recommend you begin with short moves on good holds so that you become strong enough to control the movements. Focus on landing the holds with your elbows slightly bent and work on not extending your arms fully. Tighten up your body and focus especially on your core, as it's important to maintain tension in order to avoid unnecessary rotations.

NUMBER OF MOVES PER PROBLEM: 4 to 8
REST: minimum 3 minutes
NUMBER OF TRIES IN TOTAL: 9 total, on 3 separate problems
WALL ANGLE: 40 degrees and steeper
HOLDS: varied

PROW

If your local climbing wall has a prow, climbing it without using your feet will be good compression strength training. Use sloping holds that require you to squeeze and press your hands in towards each other in order to hang on.

SLOW **MOVES**

Use good holds and do the moves as slowly as you can. The focus here is on arm and upper body strength.

 You should be able to do five pull-ups before you start campus training.

SHORT **MOVES**

Use closely spaced bad holds in order to train finger strength. The focus here is not on pulling far or creating speed, but rather on using holds so small they barely enable you to hang on and move between them.

 It's best to find a really steep wall to begin with. The less steep the wall, the more you will have to pull up for each move, and that's exactly what makes this hard.

COMPRESSION

Compressing between holds is when you're squeezing the palms of your hands towards each other against opposite-facing hold surfaces. The compression disappears when you let go with one hand, so you quickly have to move to the next hold to regain the compression between the holds. This places special demands on your upper body strength and should be trained specifically. In this exercise we therefore want you to choose, or make up, different boulder problems where you actively have to work with compression. If you choose holds on each side of a prow or an edge this will usually involve compression, and so this is a good place to start.

NUMBER OF MOVES PER PROBLEM: 6 to 8
REST: minimum 3 minutes
NUMBER OF TRIES IN TOTAL: 15 total, on 3 to 5 separate problems
WALL ANGLE: vertical to roof
HOLDS: hold surfaces that face away from each other; slopers will be the most effective

PULLING THROUGH

We're all familiar with the feeling of landing a hold, but not being able to pull through to the next. Sometimes we're able to match, but it is an extremely valuable physical ability to be able to pull through using just one arm. You can train this by doing long moves on relatively good holds, while avoiding matching. Then you can train pulling through on one arm for every move.

NUMBER OF MOVES PER PROBLEM: 6 to 8
REST: minimum 3 minutes
NUMBER OF TRIES IN TOTAL: 15 total, on 3 to 5 separate problems
WALL ANGLE: 15 to 60 degrees overhanging
HOLDS: good holds

POSITIONING EXERCISES

BY CLIMBING ON boulder problems that consist solely or mostly of either undercuts, sidepulls or upward-facing holds, you can specifically address the requirements for positioning that these holds force you to consider. When you begin this training we recommend using relatively good holds, so that the focus of your training is on your arms, upper body and core. You can narrow this focus down even further by choosing steeper walls. Then you can move on to less steep walls and poorer holds to shift the focus towards finger strength, before finally being strong enough to combine small holds and steep walls. Most boulder problems and routes will require you to adapt to multiple different positions, but you can train each part specifically as described in the following exercises.

PHOTO: ISAK HUNGNES
Martin Mobråten sending *Shantaram* (Font 8b+/c) on Ramsøya outside of Vingsand, Norway.

FRONTING

Choose holds that are positioned as close to horizontal on the wall as possible. Eliminate all other techniques, like twisting in, and heel and toe hooks, and perform every move as controlled as you can while fronting the wall. This requires strength in your arms and shoulders, because your arms are angled away from the wall. The wider the positions and the greater the distance between the holds, the harder the exercise will be. You should therefore vary the distance between the holds both vertically and horizontally.

NUMBER OF MOVES PER PROBLEM: 6 to 8
REST: minimum 3 minutes
NUMBER OF TRIES IN TOTAL: 15 total, on 3 to 5 separate problems
WALL ANGLE: vertical to 60 degrees overhanging
HOLDS: positive and relatively good holds

 Remember your pinkie! Use four fingers on the hold as this will automatically activate the shoulder and arm to a greater extent.

TWISTING IN

Choose sidepulls that are as close to vertical as possible and twist in for every move. This means twisting your right hip in towards the wall when moving your right arm, and vice versa.

NUMBER OF MOVES PER PROBLEM: 6 to 8
REST: minimum 3 minutes
NUMBER OF TRIES IN TOTAL: 15 total, on 3 to 5 separate problems
WALL ANGLE: vertical to 60 degrees overhanging
HOLDS: positive and relatively good holds

GASTON

Choose holds where the grip surface is facing in towards the middle, and do every move as a shoulder press, or gaston. The more vertical the holds, the harder the moves will be. You can either front or twist in, but your arm and hand will be working in the same position the whole time.

NUMBER OF MOVES PER PROBLEM: 6 to 8
REST: minimum 3 minutes
NUMBER OF TRIES IN TOTAL: 15 total, on 3 to 5 separate problems
WALL ANGLE: vertical to 60 degrees overhanging
HOLDS: positive and relatively good holds

LOCKING OFF

In many cases, handholds can be so small, undefined or bad that it's hard to land them correctly when carrying too much speed. Therefore, it's important to have the necessary strength to be able to lock off in your arms and body to grab the next hold in control. Choose a steep boulder problem on good holds. Lock off for 2 to 3 seconds with your free hand hovering just above the next hold before grabbing it, and repeat this for every move.

NUMBER OF MOVES PER PROBLEM: 4 to 8
REST: minimum 3 minutes
NUMBER OF TRIES IN TOTAL: 15 total, on 3 to 5 separate problems
WALL ANGLE: vertical to 60 degrees overhanging
HOLDS: positive and relatively good holds

TURTLE

We are stronger in some body positions and at some arm angles than others. By moving to the next hold at a steady pace you can train the parts of the movement where you aren't as strong. The holds should be relatively good, so that you're able to pull through the move in a steady and controlled fashion. Focus on moving at roughly the same speed throughout the entire move.

NUMBER OF MOVES PER PROBLEM: 6 to 8
REST: minimum 3 minutes
NUMBER OF TRIES IN TOTAL: 10 total, on 2 to 3 separate problems
WALL ANGLE: vertical to 60 degrees overhanging
HOLDS: positive and relatively good holds

MARKING

Marking holds with your feet is a good way to train your core, in addition to it being hard for your arms. Choose steep walls and make up a boulder problem with good holds. Cut your feet loose and touch the next handhold with one of your feet. Place your feet back down on the footholds you were standing on and then move to the next hold. Repeat for every move.

NUMBER OF MOVES PER PROBLEM: 4 to 6
REST: minimum 3 minutes
NUMBER OF TRIES IN TOTAL: 10 total, on 2 to 3 separate problems
WALL ANGLE: 60 degrees overhanging to roof
HOLDS: jugs

 If it's too difficult to cut your feet loose, you can walk them up to the hold you're aiming for by using any and all footholds, and then walk them back down.

HANG ON

Taking a swing is hard work for the whole body. The quicker you can stop it, the better your chances are of hanging on to the holds. After stopping the swing, you then have to get your feet back on to the wall, which is yet another hard move. This exercise trains both parts.

Use holds on a steep wall or a lip.* Swing your feet in and stop the movement by placing your feet on one or two footholds; hold this position for a few seconds. Cut your feet loose and repeat. Make the exercise harder by using poorer holds or by increasing the distance between the handholds and footholds.

* A lip is the edge between two wall angles, for example when a roof transitions over to a vertical wall.

NUMBER OF MOVES PER PROBLEM: 6 to 8 swings
REST: minimum 3 minutes
NUMBER OF SETS: 4 to 6
WALL ANGLE: 45 degrees to roof
HOLDS: varied

ON THE LIMIT
As the title implies, you'll be climbing boulder problems that are at the limit of your ability. The possibilities are endless in terms of wall angles, grip types, grip size and lengths of moves. This is a good opportunity to climb problems with different themes, as described earlier in the book, and

be conscious of how you train your strengths, weaknesses, or even both in one session.

NUMBER OF MOVES PER PROBLEM: 3 to 6
REST: minimum 4 minutes
NUMBER OF TRIES IN TOTAL: 10 total, on 2 to 3 separate problems
WALL ANGLE: 15 degrees overhanging to roof
HOLDS: varied

 You should make up and try problems in advance so that you know they are at the right level for the session, and so that you know them well enough to have consistently good, high-quality tries.

AMERICAN STYLE

'American style' is a dynamic climbing style with lots of big moves, dynos and swings. You should create a lot of speed from down low and land the next hold with your arms bent. Sticking the hold and taking the swing will be the hardest part, and you should focus on keeping your arms bent and making the swing as short as possible. This exercise requires a great deal of strength in the arms, upper body, stomach and back. We recommend starting off with fewer moves per problem to consistently maintain a high quality for every move.

NUMBER OF MOVES PER PROBLEM: 3 to 6
REST: minimum 4 minutes
NUMBER OF TRIES IN TOTAL: 15 total, on 2 to 3 separate problems
WALL ANGLE: 45 to 60 degrees overhanging
HOLDS: positive holds

POWER EXERCISES

JUMP START

How fast you're able to close your hand as you grab a hold and how fast you're able to stop your body's momentum are important abilities when it comes to hard climbing, and especially bouldering. For this exercise you'll start standing on the ground. Grab a hold with one hand and jump to another hold with your free hand. Work on landing the next hold with your arms slightly bent, and stiffen your body from your fingertips and throughout your whole upper body as you land the hold. The hold you're jumping to should be so bad that you're only just able to stop the momentum and hold the position for 2 to 3 seconds. To make the exercise harder, you can choose poorer holds or increase the distance between them.

NUMBER OF MOVES PER PROBLEM: 1
NUMBER OF TRIES IN TOTAL: 9 per hand, on 3 separate problems
REST: 5 seconds between each jump, 2 minutes between each problem
WALL ANGLE: 15 to 60 degrees overhanging
HOLDS: varied

Kick start

VARIATIONS:
- You can start with both one hand and one foot on the wall and kick. This is what we call a 'kick start' and it will make it easier to increase the distance to the hold you're aiming for. Kick starts often require a higher degree of finger and upper body strength than a jump start.
- You can also jump from the ground with both hands to one or two holds. As you land the hold, or holds, they should be so bad that you're only just able to stop the momentum and hold the position for 2 to 3 seconds. You can start by jumping straight up, but after a while you can try to start from slightly further in, forcing you to jump backwards. This will increase the swing which will be harder to hold.

 As you become strong enough, the best way to do the exercise is by jumping to edges or pinches.

Jump start

DYNOS

Unlike the jump start and kick start, you now have to create the upwards momentum from a position on the wall. This movement is much more technically complicated and will also demand more pulling strength from the arms and upper body in the starting phase. Additionally, it will require strength in the fingers and arms/upper body as you land the hold you're aiming for. The steeper the wall, the harder it gets. Start on vertical walls and work your way up from there.

THREE POINTS OFF

Start from good holds and dyno to a hold you might struggle a bit to hold, while not letting go with your lower hand. Work on landing the move with your arms slightly bent and stopping your body's momentum. Sticking the upper hold will require finger strength, and landing with your arms bent and stopping the swing will require arm and upper body strength. To increase the difficulty of this exercise you can make both the start holds and the hold you're dynoing to poorer, and then you can increase the distance between them.

NUMBER OF MOVES PER PROBLEM: 1

NUMBER OF TRIES IN TOTAL: 9 per hand, on 3 separate problems
REST: 10 to 20 seconds between each dyno, 2 minutes between each problem
WALL ANGLE: 15 to 60 degrees overhanging
HOLDS: varied starting and top holds

ALL POINTS OFF

Start from bad holds in a challenging starting position and dyno as far as you can to the next hold. The hold you're aiming for can be a good one, and you can lose all points of contact except the arm you're landing with.

The focus is on creating momentum from a challenging, finger-intensive position. Getting established in the starting position will require finger strength, and initiating the dyno will require power in the rest of your body.

NUMBER OF MOVES PER PROBLEM: 1
NUMBER OF TRIES IN TOTAL: 9 per hand, on 3 separate problems
REST: 10 to 20 seconds between each dyno, 2 minutes between each problem
WALL ANGLE: 15 to 40 degrees overhanging
HOLDS: poor starting holds, good top holds

KANGAROO

Start with good holds and dyno as high as you can. Focus on covering as much distance as possible; you don't need to land and hang on to the next hold. This requires power in your arms, upper body and legs.

NUMBER OF MOVES PER PROBLEM: 1
NUMBER OF TRIES IN TOTAL: 9 tries, on 3 separate problems
REST: 10 to 20 seconds between each dyno, 2 minutes between each problem
WALL ANGLE: 10 to 40 degrees overhanging

HOLDS: good

MONKEY

Start with good holds, dyno as high as you can and land with either one or two hands on a good hold. This requires power in your arms, upper body and legs.

NUMBER OF MOVES PER PROBLEM: 1
NUMBER OF TRIES IN TOTAL: 12 tries, on 3 separate problems
REST: 1 minute rest between each dyno
WALL ANGLE: 10 to 40 degrees overhanging
HOLDS: good

CAMPUSING

We have already described [footless climbing](#) for strength training. The focus for this exercise is to make the moves as big as possible and do them as quickly as possible. This will require rapid force development in both the start and end phases of the move.

GO BIG

Do big moves on good holds. Work on creating a lot of speed and landing with your arms bent. It's better to start with your arms relatively level in order to create an explosive move. You can therefore go big with one hand, match it with your other hand and then go big again with your other hand.

NUMBER OF MOVES PER PROBLEM: 2 to 4
REST: 3 minutes
NUMBER OF TRIES IN TOTAL: 9 to 12 tries, on 3 to 4 separate problems
WALL ANGLE: 45 degrees overhanging to roof
HOLDS: jugs and positive edges and pinches

GO FAST

Do relatively short and simple campus moves as quickly as you can. Time yourself and try to improve every try. When your time starts to slow down, your set is complete.

NUMBER OF MOVES PER PROBLEM: 4 to 6
REST: 3 minutes
NUMBER OF TRIES IN TOTAL: 9 to 12 tries, on 3 to 4 separate problems
WALL ANGLE: 45 degrees overhanging to roof
HOLDS: jugs

ISOLATED STRENGTH EXERCISES

THERE ARE MANY advantages to training strength on the climbing wall, but some physical properties are so essential that it can be a good idea to complement our training with some isolated exercises. This gives us the opportunity to target a select few elements at a time in a controlled fashion, and this might yield better results than if we were to train them in combination with other elements. We recommend isolated exercises for finger, arm and core strength to improve performance on the wall and to reduce the risk of injury.

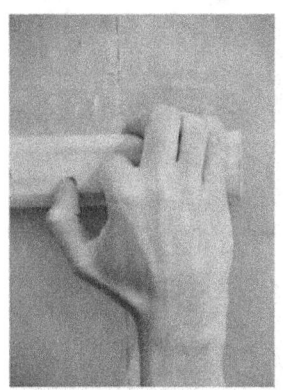
Back three

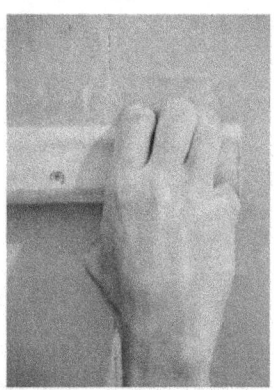
Front three

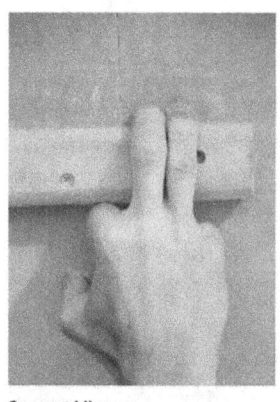
Open middle two

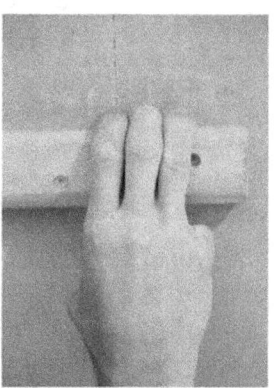
Open front three

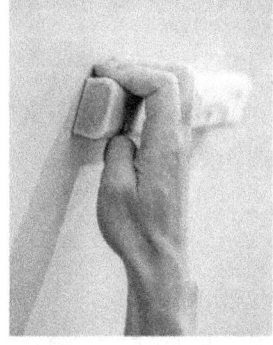
Half crimp

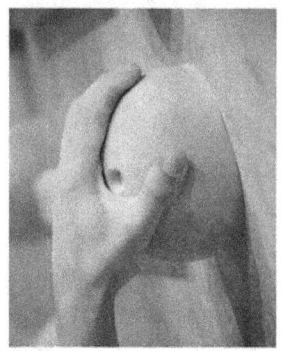
Sloper

DEADHANGS
As we wrote in *The Climbing Bible*, deadhangs are one of the most specific

and controllable methods we have for training finger strength. Previously, specific finger training has been considered very risky with regard to sustaining finger injuries, both for younger and older climbers, but this entirely comes down to the training method and how high the training dosage is. Finger strength training can be done using safe and controlled methods, which, all in all, will put the climber at a lower risk of injury than a regular climbing session. In addition, systematic finger strength training will over time also strengthen muscles, tendons, joints and ligaments, further reducing the risk of injury. What's important is to conduct the training with proper technique and in control, and focus on the training dosage – as in how much and how hard you train per session, per week, and over a longer period.

In *The Climbing Bible* we presented a small selection of exercises for finger strength training. Here we present further methods for training different properties, to ensure progression and variation in your finger strength training.

If you were to choose to train only one grip position, we recommend training using the half crimp. This is more usable for most holds and is also more specific than the open-handed grip when it comes to using small holds, something which is usually the case when it comes to hard climbing. Still, it's wise to vary the grip positions so that you also become stronger when using an open-handed grip, and on slopers and pockets. The following exercises can be done using any grip position, but unless another grip position is specifically mentioned we recommend the half crimp as the standard grip position.

UNLOADING

In principle, anyone can train deadhangs, it's just a question of how much they need to unload from their body weight. For example, a climber weighing 70 kilograms can unload 35 kilograms and thereby train at half their body weight. This will allow them to train effectively and with control, focusing on proper technical execution and at a lower risk of injury compared to regular climbing. As you get more comfortable with the hanging position and can do each hang with a slight margin – meaning you can hang significantly longer than the number of seconds described for each exercise – you can gradually decrease the number of deloaded kilograms to ensure you're training at the correct load. In order to unload some body weight, we recommend using a simple pulley system with a harness and weights, as demonstrated in this photo.

 Remember to pull your shoulders down and rotate your elbows slightly in towards each other.

TORTURE HANGS

The goal for this exercise is to hang for 30 to 40 seconds per hang. Choose a grip position or an edge depth that only just enables you to hang for 30 to 40 seconds. If you can hang for more than 40 seconds, use poorer holds. You can start by hanging from a pull-up bar or from jugs and gradually work your way to hanging from poorer holds. Complete four to six hangs with a 2- to 3-minute rest between each hang.

HANG TIME: 30 to 40 seconds
NUMBER OF HANGS PER SET: 1
NUMBER OF SETS: 4 to 6
REST BETWEEN SETS: 2 to 3 minutes
MARGIN[*]: none

[*] By *margin*, we mean how much longer you *could* have hung. If we say you should have

a 3-second margin for a hang that should last 10 seconds, you should let go after 10 seconds, but have enough margin that you could have hung on for an additional 3 seconds. No margin means hang until exhaustion, meaning you're unable to hang on any longer.

REPEATERS 1

Choose four or five different grip positions, for example four finger half crimp, sloper, front three open grip and front three half crimp. Complete the following for each grip position: hang for 7 seconds, rest for 3 seconds, and do seven hangs, so that you're near exhaustion for the last (seventh) hang. Take a 2- to 3-minute rest and repeat for the remaining grip positions.

HANG TIME: 7 seconds
REST BETWEEN HANGS: 3 seconds
NUMBER OF HANGS PER SET: 7
NUMBER OF SETS: 4 or 5
REST BETWEEN SETS: 2 to 3 minutes
MARGIN: near exhaustion for the last hang of each set

REPEATERS 2

Choose one grip position which you wish to improve and do the following: hang for 10 seconds, rest for 5 seconds, and do four hangs, so that you're near exhaustion for the last hang. Take a 3- to 5-minute rest and complete another three sets. This is supposed to be a more challenging exercise than *Repeaters 1*, so the holds should be poorer, or you should unload less weight from or add more weight to your body weight.

HANG TIME: 10 seconds
REST BETWEEN HANGS: 5 seconds
NUMBER OF HANGS PER SET: 4
NUMBER OF SETS: 4
REST BETWEEN SETS: 3 to 5 minutes
MARGIN: near exhaustion for the last hang of each set

MAXIMUM WEIGHT

Start with relatively deep edges so that you're able to add extra weight. Use the half crimp and do the following: hang for 10 seconds, rest for 3 minutes, and do five hangs in total. Keep a margin of 1 to 3 seconds for each hang, so that you're able to maintain good grip and body posture throughout the whole hang, and so you can put your feet back on the ground while still in control after 10 seconds. If you're able to hang for more than 13 seconds you can add more weight.

HANG TIME: 10 seconds
NUMBER OF HANGS PER SET: 1
NUMBER OF SETS: 5
REST BETWEEN SETS: 3 minutes
MARGIN: 1 to 3 seconds

SHALLOW EDGE

Hang using a half crimp grip from the shallowest edges possible. Do the following: hang for 10 seconds, rest for 3 minutes, and do five hangs in total. Keep a margin of 1 to 3 seconds for each hang, so that you're able to maintain good grip and body posture throughout the whole hang, and so you can put your feet back on the ground while still in control after 10 seconds. If you're able to hang for more than 13 seconds you can choose an even shallower edge.

HANG TIME: 10 seconds
NUMBER OF HANGS PER SET: 1
NUMBER OF SETS: 5
REST BETWEEN SETS: 3 minutes
MARGIN: 1 to 3 seconds

SHORT AND HARD

This exercise can be done with either one or two hands, and with either added weight on deeper edges or without any added weight on as shallow edges as possible. Do the following: hang for 3 to 5 seconds, rest for 1 minute, and do six hangs in total. Focus on developing as much force as possible in the shortest amount of time, meaning you should pull as hard as you can for every hang. If you're able to hang for more than 5 seconds you will either have to add more weight, or make the hold worse, or remove some of the weight if you're deloading.

HANG TIME: 3 to 5 seconds
NUMBER OF HANGS PER SET: 1
NUMBER OF SETS: 6

REST BETWEEN SETS: 1 minute
MARGIN: none

DEADHANGS

For experienced climbers who have been doing a lot of deadhang training with both hands, the one-handed deadhang can be the next natural step forward. Even if you're able to hang at full body weight from just one hand, we want to emphasise the usefulness of deloading. Hanging from one hand is a different technique than hanging from both, and it's wise to start with the right amount of deloading to make sure you're executing the exercise correctly and with control. Since your body will start to rotate around your arm when you're hanging from one hand, your free hand should be used to stop this rotation so that you're hanging without your body moving at all.

PHOTO: MARTIN MOBRÅTEN
Stian Christophersen sends *Power of Landjager* (Font 8a), Hueco Tanks, USA. Training both deadhangs and one-arm lock-offs can help you control your body's rotation and pull through with one arm without having to match.

EXERCISES USING A PORTABLE FINGERBOARD

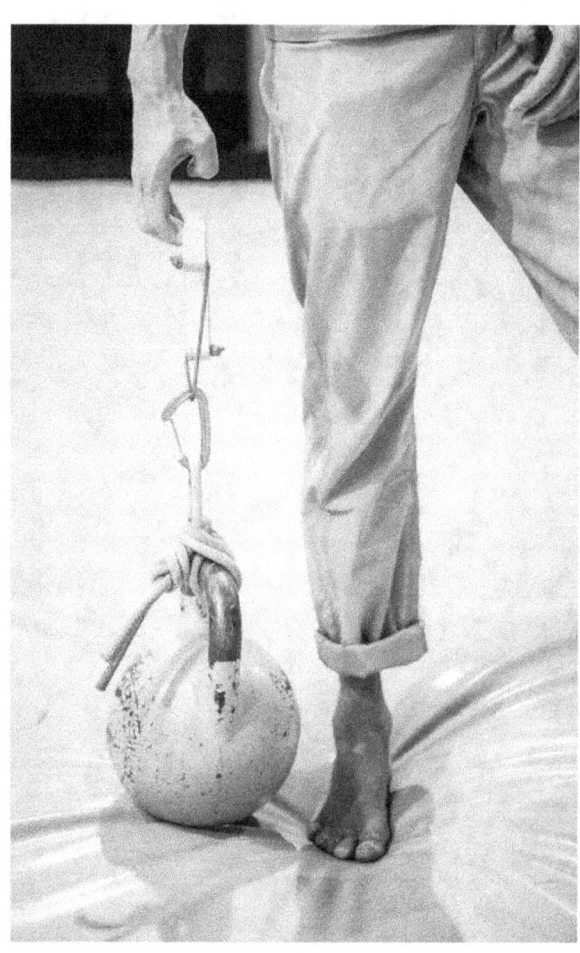 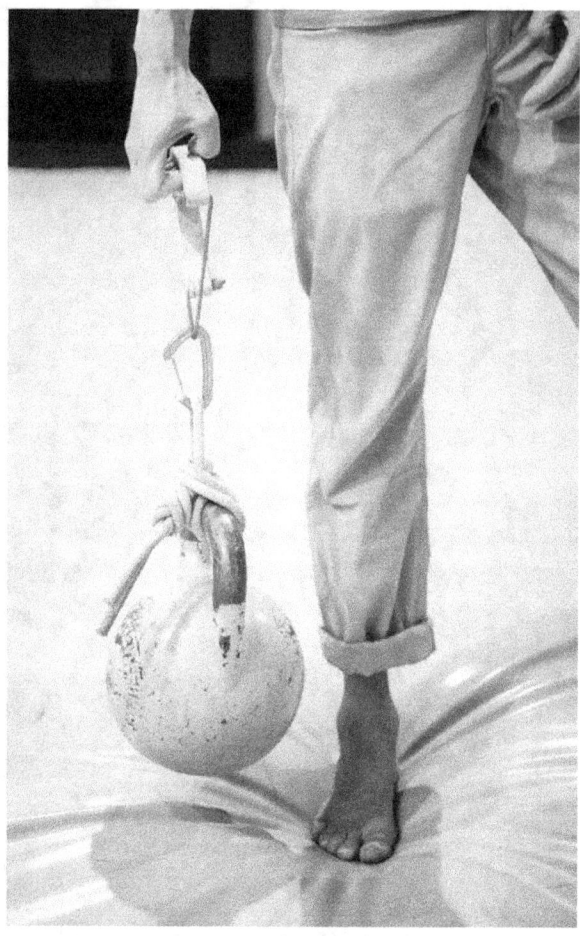

THERE ARE SEVERAL portable fingerboard solutions if you're on a trip somewhere or for some other reason don't have access to a regular mounted fingerboard. All deadhang exercises can of course be done on these boards, but they will move about more as you hang from them. Another option is to attach weights to the end of the board and lift them instead. This will allow you to easily see how many kilograms you're able to load with. By doing it this way you can also use the same training methods as described in this chapter, although we recommend training one hand at a time so that you don't have to add so much weight.

Another training method that's suitable for portable boards is *finger curls*. This means starting in an open grip position and curling your fingers up into a crimp. This is dynamic strength training for your finger musculature and it's a good supplement to the more classic and static deadhang exercises. Do the following:

Find the load (number of kilograms) you're able to curl from an open hand into a crimp, such that you are near exhaustion after eight repetitions. Complete three sets per hand with a 3-minute rest between each set.

NUMBER OF CURLS PER SET: 8
NUMBER OF SETS: 3
REST BETWEEN SETS: 3 minutes
MARGIN PER SET: 1 RIR*

* Repetition in reserve (RIR) is used as a measurement of intensity in dynamic strength training. It refers to how many more repetitions you feel you would be able to complete in a set. If RIR = 0 you're completely exhausted. The higher your RIR per set is, the further away you are from exhaustion. For strength training to have an effect on the force development in a muscle, your RIR should be no higher than 5.

Start with less added weight than you think. This is a very hard exercise.

JUMP TO THE EDGE

An obvious factor for whether we're able to do a move or not, is how fast we're able to close our grip around the hold we're aiming for. This ability – being able to grip hard and fast – is probably more important in bouldering than in route climbing, but will in many instances be the deciding factor at the crux of a route. Earlier in the chapter we described how this ability can be trained through the 'jump start' and the 'kick start', and we can do exactly the same exercise on the campus board.

VERSION 1

Hold a rung at shoulder height with one hand and jump as high as you can with the other hand in such a way that you're able to land the next rung with your arm slightly bent. Hold this position for 2 seconds, take a 5-second rest, and repeat six to eight times per arm.

VERSION 2

Jump from the ground and grab a rung with both arms slightly bent. Hold the position for 2 seconds, take a 5-second rest, and repeat six to eight times.

VERSION 3

Stand facing sideways to the campus board, jump from the ground and grab a rung with one hand. Vary the angle in your elbow so that you alternate between angles from slightly bent to 90 degrees. Hold the position for 2 seconds, take a 5-second rest, and repeat six to eight times per arm.

ARM & UPPER BODY STRENGTH EXERCISES

CLIMBING IS A *pulling-based* sport, and as the walls become steeper and the moves become longer, we are dependent on increasing our pulling strength. In this book we have deliberately planned for most of the arm and upper body strength training to take place on the climbing wall. Still, it can be appropriate to supplement this with some isolated pulling strength exercises, in different controlled and varied ways.

LOCK-OFFS
TWO-HANDED LOCK-OFFS
Hang from a bar or two jugs using both hands and with your arms bent. Hang until you're unable to hold the position. If you can't hold this position for more than a few seconds we recommend deloading using an elastic band or a pulley system, so that you're able to hang for around 10 seconds. Work your way up to hanging for 30 seconds. If you're able to hang for significantly longer than this, we recommend adding extra weight or moving on to one-handed lock-offs. You can alternate between using overhand and underhand grips, and vary the angle of your elbows – how bent your arms are. We recommend training at different angles, from your elbows bent at 90 degrees to your arms almost fully extended.

HANG TIME: 30 seconds
NUMBER OF HANGS PER SET: 1
NUMBER OF SETS: 4 to 6
REST BETWEEN SETS: 2 minutes
MARGIN PER HANG: 2 to 3 seconds

ONE-HANDED LOCK-OFFS, TORTURE HANGS

Position yourself sideways with one hand on a bar or a jug, and your arm bent. In this exercise you will aim to hold this position for 15 seconds, so, if necessary, deload until this is possible. Again, we recommend training at different elbow angles, from 90 degrees to almost fully extended.

HANG TIME: 15 seconds
NUMBER OF HANGS PER SET: 1
NUMBER OF SETS: 4 per arm
REST BETWEEN SETS: 2 to 3 minutes
MARGIN PER HANG: none

ONE-HANDED LOCK-OFFS, MAX HANGS

Position yourself as per the previous exercise. You will now deload or add enough weight so that you are only just able to hang for a maximum of 5 seconds. Vary the angle of your elbows as per the previous exercise.

HANG TIME: 3 to 5 seconds
NUMBER OF HANGS PER SET: 1
NUMBER OF SETS: 6 per arm
REST BETWEEN SETS: 2 to 3 minutes
MARGIN PER HANG: 0 to 1 seconds

JUMP TO LOCK-OFF

This exercise can be done with either one or both hands. Stand on the ground and jump to a bar or a jug. Land at different elbow angles and hold the position for a couple of seconds. As a set you can do six of these jumps with a couple of seconds' rest in between each jump, and do three sets in total.

HANG TIME: 2 seconds
REST BETWEEN JUMPS: 2 to 5 seconds
NUMBER OF HANGS PER SET: 6
NUMBER OF SETS: 3
REST BETWEEN SETS: 2 minutes
MARGIN PER HANG: 1 to 3 seconds

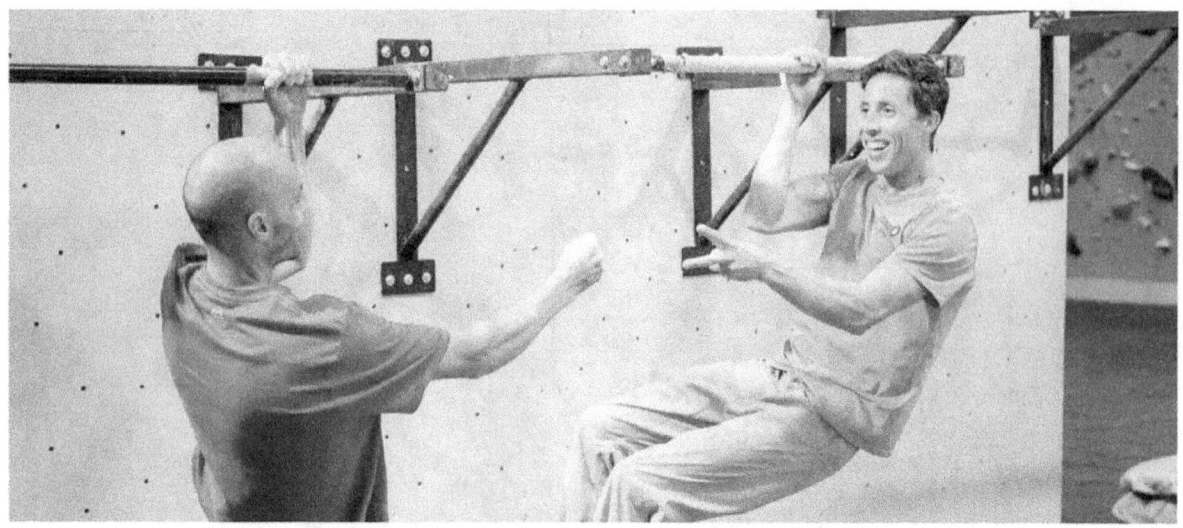

CHALLENGE

Eat a banana or a donut or drink a cup of coffee while locking off on one arm, and challenge your friends to do the same. Can you eat or drink it all, and who can manage the biggest meal or cup?

PULL-UPS

REGULAR

Start by hanging from a bar or two jugs with your arms shoulder width apart. Start the movement by rotating your arms so that the insides of your elbows are facing in towards the middle, pull your shoulder blades down and towards each other and bend your elbows so that you can pull all the way up until your chin is above your hands. It can be a good idea to start by deloading a bit of weight to learn the technique properly and to increase the number of repetitions per set.

REPETITIONS: 8 to 12
NUMBER OF SETS: 3
REST BETWEEN SETS: 3 minutes
SPEED: calm and even throughout the movement
MARGIN PER SET: <3 RIR

WEIGHTED

When you're able to do regular pull-ups and have a good margin for each of the three sets at 12 repetitions, a natural progression is to make each repetition harder and reduce the number of repetitions. Ideally you will have tested what your maximum strength is for one repetition (known as one rep maximum, or 1RM) and will perform each set with a load that is above 85 percent of that. If you haven't tested your maximum strength, you can use RIR as a measurement, and for this exercise you shouldn't have more than one repetition in reserve per set.

REPETITIONS: 4
NUMBER OF SETS: 4
REST BETWEEN SETS: 3 minutes
SPEED: try to pull as hard and fast as possible, even if the weight makes you move slowly
MARGIN PER SET: 0 to 1 RIR

JERKS

The goal here is to complete each repetition as fast as possible. Start with your arms slightly bent and pull up as fast as you can, then slowly lower down and repeat. To stimulate the speed, you can deload using an elastic band to achieve so-called *superspeed*, and thereby achieve a higher speed throughout the movement.

REPETITIONS: 3 to 6
NUMBER OF SETS: 4
REST BETWEEN SETS: 3 minutes
SPEED: as fast as possible
MARGIN PER SET: you want to have margin to complete a lot more repetitions, but should complete the set when the speed drops

NEGATIVE

A negative pull-up is when you lower from the top position down on to straight arms. This involves slowing down the movement instead of initiating it – so-called eccentric training. For less experienced climbers this can be a good supplement to doing your first pull-up, while more experienced and stronger climbers can use negative pull-ups as a good method to aggressively stimulate muscle growth and take further steps in their training. It's important to remember that eccentric training is quite a strenuous form of training which can lead to severe muscle soreness, so be careful.

REPETITIONS: 2 to 8
NUMBER OF SETS: 3
REST BETWEEN SETS: 3 minutes
SPEED: calm and controlled throughout the movement
MARGIN PER SET: 1 to 2 RIR

As an example, start with one to two repetitions in sets of three once per week, and gradually increase to eight repetitions in sets of three, twice per week.

ARCHER PULL-UPS

Pull up and lock off in the top position. Move from side to side while alternating straightening out your arms. This means your bent arm will have to take most of your weight while your other arm is straight.

REPETITIONS: 4
NUMBER OF SETS: 4
REST BETWEEN SETS: 3 minutes
SPEED: calm and controlled throughout the movement
MARGIN PER SET: 2 RIR

CLAP

Do a pull-up as fast as you can, let go at the top of the movement and clap your hands. Vary the angle you land in – the longer you're in the air, the less bend you will have in your elbows as you land.

REPETITIONS: 4 to 6

NUMBER OF SETS: 3
REST BETWEEN SETS: 3 minutes
SPEED: as fast as possible
MARGIN PER SET: you want to have margin to complete a lot more repetitions, but should complete the set when the speed drops

ONE-ARM PULL-UP

Position yourself sideways below the bar and do a one-arm pull-up. We recommend first deloading to properly learn the technique and maintain control throughout the movement. A pulley system is ideal as it will ensure an even load throughout the movement.

REPETITIONS: 2 per arm
NUMBER OF SETS: 4 per arm

REST BETWEEN SETS: 3 minutes
SPEED: calm and controlled throughout the movement
MARGIN PER SET: 1 RIR

COMBINATIONS

In addition to training both finger strength and arm/upper body strength individually, it's good to combine them in the same exercise. We can do this by doing pull-ups on varied grips and in different positions, or through campus training.

FINGERBOARD PULL-UPS

Vary the grip positions for each set, so that you train pull-ups on edges, pockets and slopers. The holds should be so bad that you're unable to do more than four to six repetitions per set, and because they are are bad you will need to remain calm and in control so that you don't slide off the holds.

REPETITIONS: 4 to 6
NUMBER OF SETS: 3
REST BETWEEN SETS: 3 minutes
SPEED: calm and controlled throughout the movement
MARGIN PER SET: 0 to 1 RIR
GRIP TYPE: varied

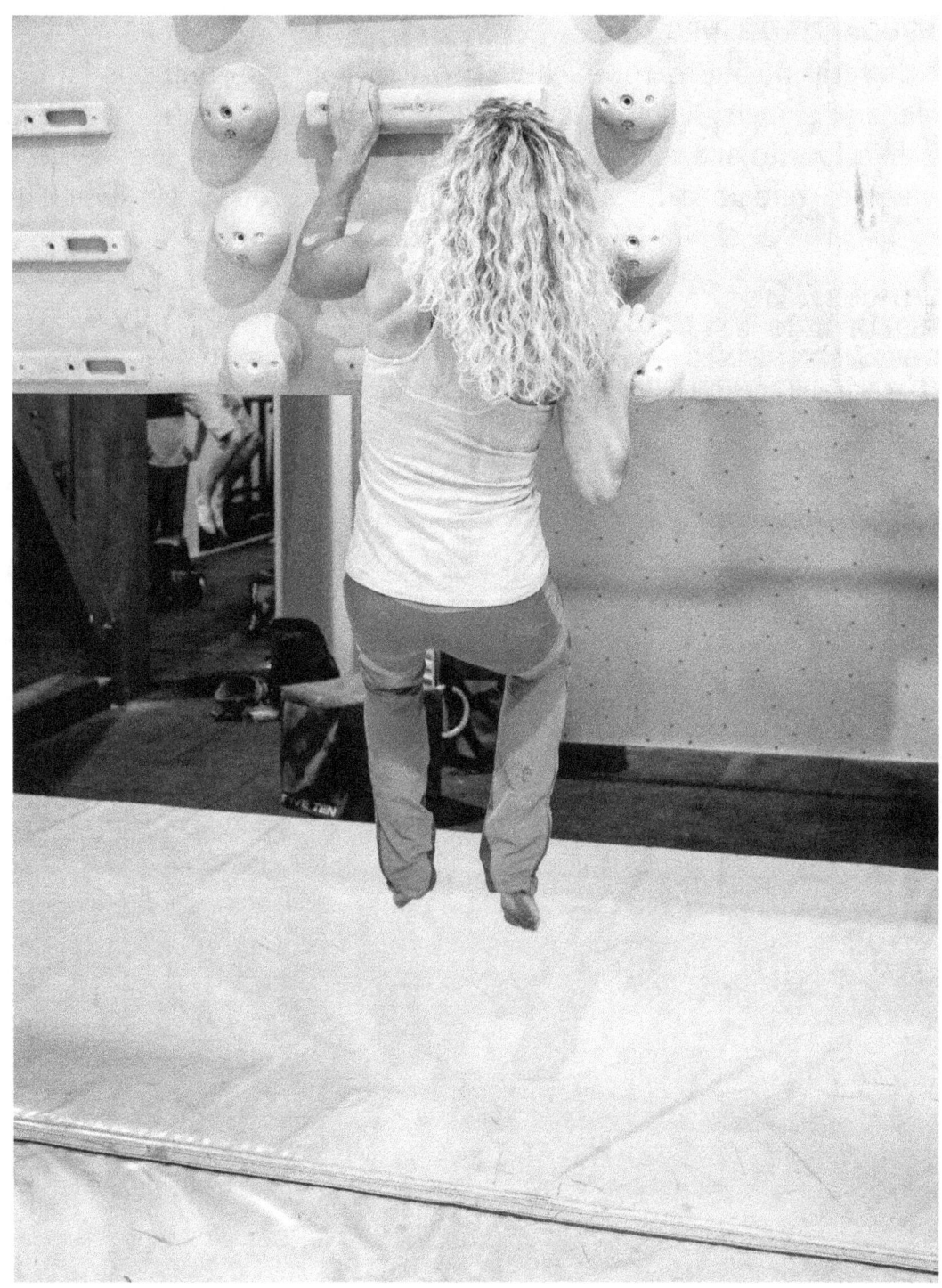

OFFSET

Offset means your hands are gripping holds at different heights. This is in many ways closer to the movement pattern we face while climbing and therefore it's a good exercise for training pulling strength in different positions. The bigger the difference in width and height between the holds, the harder the exercise will be. We also recommend varying the grip type used for the exercise. If, for example, you want to train pinches, choose pinches for both hands. You can also choose a poorer hold for the upper hand and a jug for the lower hand, and vice versa, to vary which part of the movement is the hardest.

REPETITIONS: 4 to 8
NUMBER OF SETS: 3
REST BETWEEN SETS: 3 minutes
SPEED: calm and controlled throughout the movement
MARGIN PER SET: 0 to 1 RIR
GRIP TYPE: varied

CAMPUS

For fully grown climbers, it's possible to keep campus training as a relatively safe training method by learning proper technique and maintaining a reasonable progression. First and foremost, it's important to learn the moves on the campus board, and for most climbers the best way to do this is to stand on footholds below the board and practise the moves.

It's natural to begin with shorter moves on the best campus rungs, and then increase the distance between the rungs before finally moving on to shallower rungs as you gain control.

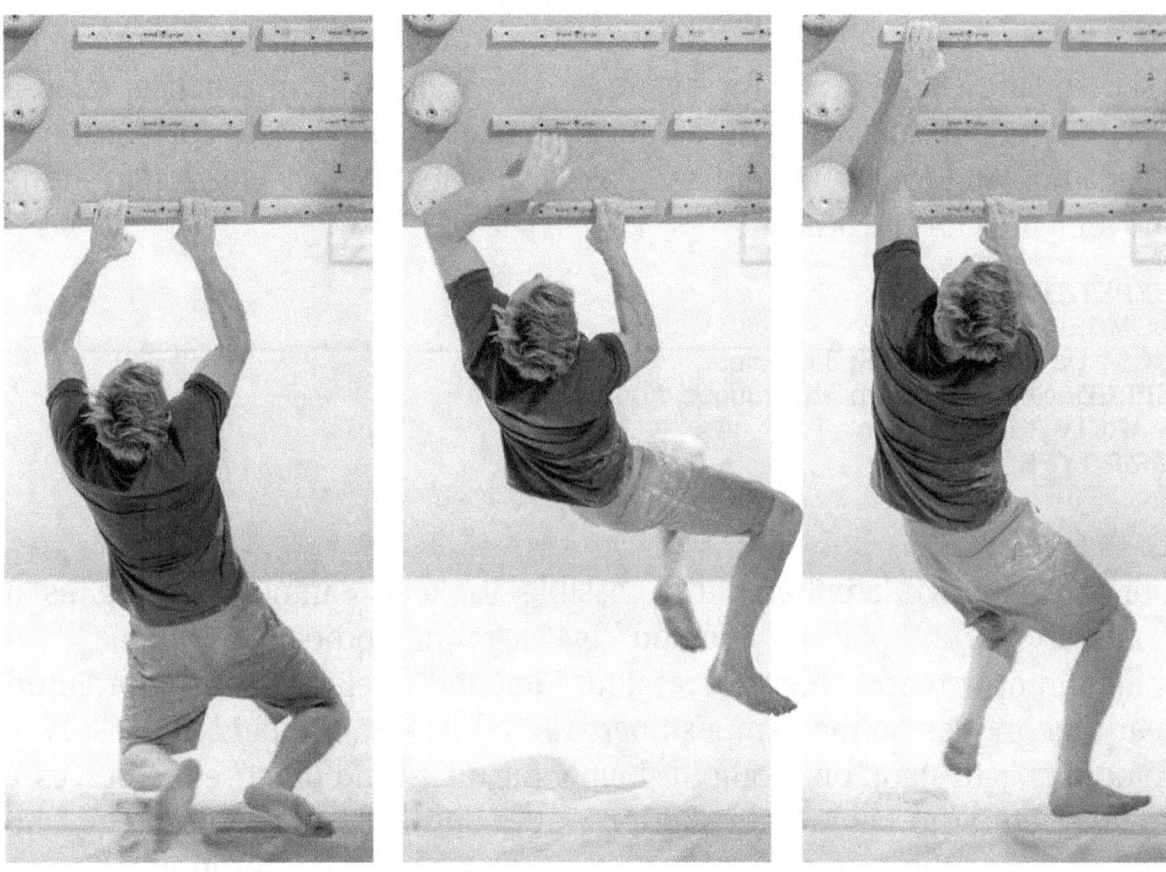

STRENGTH

Campus training is an effective method for training finger strength as well as arm and upper body strength, in addition to training technical elements like coordination and dynamics. To train strength and to learn the technique of the moves, we recommend starting with relatively good rungs and calm movements. After a while you can increase the distance between the rungs, before moving on to shallower rungs. A strength training session can look something like this:

Warm up by doing exercises with your feet on the wall.
START BY DOING: 1-3-5 *x*3 reps per arm, with a 60-second rest between each repetition. Rest for 3 minutes.
THEN: 1-3-6 *x*2 reps per arm, with a 60-second rest between each repetition.
FINISH WITH: 1-2-3-4-5-6-7 *x*3 reps, with a 60-second rest between each repetition.

POWER

When we use the campus board for power training and finger contact strength we wish to create as much speed and cover as much distance as possible in every move. You can start by using deep rungs and work on pulling as far as you can, then move on to shallower rungs.

START BY DOING: 1 to max height **single** x3 reps per arm with a 60-second rest between each repetition. Rest for 3 minutes.
THEN: 1 to max height **double** x6 reps with a 60-second rest between each repetition. Rest for 3 minutes.
FINISH WITH: 1-2-3-4-5-6 x3 reps at max speed, with a 60-second rest between each repetition.

DOUBLE DYNOS ON THE CAMPUS BOARD

Double-dynoing on the campus board is one of the hardest and most difficult moves we can do. Training this way can yield good results, however it is also a training method that is closely related to a risk of injury. We therefore recommend double dynos only to experienced climbers who have a well-established training foundation and who have already undergone systematic campus training at lower levels of difficulty. Young athletes should hold off campus training until they are fully grown because of the risk of injury to the bones in the fingers.

Campus training should be perfomed early in the session when you are fully warmed up, but not yet too fatigued, so you can execute the training with a high level of quality. Regular climbing should wait till after the campus training.

Quarter front

Half front

Tucked front

One-legged front

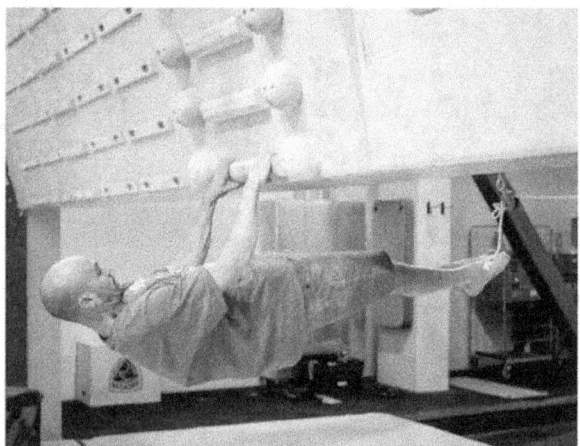
Full front

FRONT LEVER

The front lever is a classic exercise in climbing and has almost become the symbol for body strength. Through the different variations of training towards a perfect front lever, your body strength will improve. You'll become better at holding swings, better at placing your feet back on the wall, and better at maintaining body tension between your fingers and your toes. For all the variations, the goal is to maintain straight arms, pulling your chest up towards the hold, and maintaining a straight and rigid body. This becomes harder the more horizontal your body is, and therefore the natural starting point is the quarter front before moving up the ladder of difficulty to the full front. You can use hang time as a measure of intensity, and when you're able to hang in a position for 15 seconds you can move on to the next level.

HANG TIME: 5 to 15 seconds

NUMBER OF HANGS PER SET: 1
NUMBER OF SETS: 4
REST BETWEEN SETS: 2 to 3 minutes
MARGIN PER HANG: none

FRONT LEVER PULL-UP

Doing a pull-up while hanging in a front lever position is probably an exercise reserved for only the strongest among us, but it can be a nice variation to just hanging statically in the position. Doing this while in the full front lever is not only extremely hard, but also extremely difficult because of the balance of your body. If you do train the front lever pull-up, we recommend doing it while hanging in a quarter, half or tucked front lever.

REPETITIONS: 4 to 8
NUMBER OF SETS: 3

REST BETWEEN SETS: 3 minutes
SPEED: calm and controlled throughout the movement
MARGIN PER SET: 0 to 1 RIR

PHOTO: MARTIN MOBRÅTEN
Tina Johnsen Hafsaas climbing *Sin Perdón* (F8b+), Perles, Spain.

VARIATION IN TRAINING

TINA JOHNSEN HAFSAAS is Norway's best female competition climber, with a third place in the World Youth Championships and a fourth in a lead world cup as her standout results, in addition to being many times over the Norwegian and Nordic champion. She performs equally well outdoors, with multiple ascents of F8c+ routes and Font 8a+ boulder problems. Tina has been training and climbing as an elite athlete since she was only 14 years old. We asked her to share some of her thoughts around variation of specific training.

When I was 15, I was asked if I wanted to start to train. To be coached. Until then I had only climbed. I was at the climbing wall almost every day, doing what I wanted to do and what my friends did. I climbed outside when I had the chance, and had started competing abroad, but most of all I just climbed a lot. I was that young girl who could fly up most of the crimpy boulder problems but would hang for ages on routes and would struggle as soon as the climbing got physical. And people took notice. Stian grabbed me one day and asked me if I wanted a coach. I was curious and soaked it all up like a sponge. Not just from him, but from everything and everyone around me. I read a lot, asked a lot of questions and dug around wherever I could. This would turn out to be one of the biggest advantages of having a coach – having a sparring partner. Discuss, experiment, analyse, and ditch whatever didn't work. Not all the advice a small girl gets from random older men at the wall is good advice.

In terms of training we quickly addressed my physique: I had to climb steeper and harder and build a solid body that in the long term would be able to handle a lot of hard training. I had to learn to climb using four fingers and to keep my shoulder high; I had to gain the physique needed to pull through and create momentum without two holds to pull on; and I had to learn how to try really hard. We shifted most of my climbing over to steeper walls, the moves became bigger and the style more athletic. To work on the aforementioned things, new boulder problems were made that forced me to climb with four fingers and where I had to land holds with my shoulder high. Lead sessions became harder and steeper, and I continued at a high volume. After a while I was introduced to campus boarding and specific finger training, something which has been important to my development.

By mostly focusing on physical climbing, combined with a change in style in competition climbing, my weakness today is modern technique. 'New school' elements are frequently borrowed from bouldering and brought into lead climbing, and as I've grown up with steep climbing on mostly positive holds, I'm now faced with a challenge. This involves more sessions on technically challenging boulder problems, seeking out large holds where I have to position myself lower than I'm so very used to, and also spending energy and skin on pure bouldering sessions when I'm at comps and training camps abroad. This new style is here to stay. I have to adapt to it.

Over the years I've found exercises I've stuck with and always go back to, but it's still important to me to try new exercises and new training methods. Not too long ago I asked Stian why it was me he approached that time nearly 10 years ago. It was my curiosity, he replied. In hindsight, now that I'm a coach for younger athletes myself, I realise that this is exactly what is important – being curious about moves, beta, training exercises and everything else that climbing entails. And to dare. Try, fail and do better, again and again.

CHAPTER 3
CHILDREN & YOUTHS

THIS CHAPTER DESCRIBES exercises for children and youths. These exercises are designed to keep a large group active, while the coach can also follow-up individually with each climber. The chapter starts with a few thoughts on warming up before presenting examples of play-based climbing exercises you can use as a coach. Finally, more specific technical and physical exercises are presented. These are more appropriate for slightly older and more experienced children and youths.

The exercises in this chapter are a selection of the best exercises used by clubs all over Norway. We want to especially thank Oslo Climbing Club, Kolsås Climbing Club and Trondheim Climbing Club for their valuable contributions.

WARMING UP FOR CHILDREN

PHYSIOLOGICALLY, ADULT BODIES will start to prepare for an activity before getting started, through an increase in heart rate and body temperature, among other things. These changes in the transition from rest to activity are not seen in prepubescent children, and the warm-up must therefore be set up differently and last longer for children than for adults. Ideally, we want to gradually increase the level of activity, divided into short intervals of activity and rest, for a total period of 30 to 35 minutes. Since the warm-up will be a major part of the training session itself, it's important that it contains both fun and educational elements.

AREA OF FOCUS
As a coach, it's important that you have an area of focus for the session, and that all the parts of the session reflect this. If you're focusing on footwork, the general part of the warm-up should, more so than normally, activate the larger muscles in the legs. In the main part, you should choose different games and technique exercises that focus on different elements of footwork. To finish, you can gather the children and talk about what they have learned.

As with adults we start with a [general warm-up](), before moving on to a more climbing-specific part. The general part should be play based and consist of exercises that challenge both physical and mental skills, as well as coordination. Games like 'Simon says', 'red light, green light' or 'crocodile challenge' are always popular, and you can be creative and adapt the exercises to your group. In the climbing-specific part, we preserve the playfulness while introducing exercises that primarily encourage activity on the wall but also focus on technical elements like footwork, weight transfer and balance.

CLIMBING GAMES

HERE ARE SOME examples of climbing games. Mix them up to stimulate variation in the training, but return to some of them on a regular basis. Your group is guaranteed to have a favourite, and kids like repetition and predictability.

SHARK ATTACK

All the children start sitting on the mats at an equal distance from the wall. When you call out 'shark attack', everybody should climb on to the wall as quickly as possible. The last one to leave the floor gets eaten by the shark.

 Make up variations around the same theme. For example, a tsunami could mean they have to climb higher up the wall, or a storm might mean everybody has to get back down on to the mats again.

THE KING COMMANDS

All the children should start on the wall, preferably on a slab or a vertical section. They now have to do exactly what you tell them to do. If your command is to move their right hand, they have to do so, and if your command is to touch their right foot with their left hand, they have to do so. Your only limitation is your own imagination. You can adjust the level of difficulty by placing the children in different locations.

> Be inventive and add technique training to the exercises. For example, have the children look at the footholds and hover their foot above the foothold for 2 seconds to train footwork precision. You can also command them to only use sidepulls in order to train balance.

THE FLOOR IS LAVA

The floor (or matting) is lava, and the children have to traverse from a defined starting point to a defined target, without falling into the lava. You can add a few safe 'islands' where they can rest before continuing climbing so that everybody can experience a feeling of mastery on their own terms.

 Prepare the session in advance by taping a start and a finish. For the islands, you can use hula hoops or something similar on the ground.

PASSING

Divide the group into two and have one half start at the right-hand end of the wall and climb to the left. The other group starts at the opposite end and climbs to the right. They now have to pass each other on the wall. It's important that they don't climb above or below one other, as this might cause dangerous fall situations.

 To make it extra challenging, tape an upper and a lower limit they have to stay within. You can also tape holds or zones where they are allowed to pass each other. This forces the children to plan and work together to solve the task.

TARGET PRACTICE

Each child gets a ball or a beanbag and has to climb on to the wall and aim for a target on the ground. A rope bag can be a suitable target. When they have thrown the ball they have to climb back down, retrieve the ball, climb back up and throw again. Give the group 1 minute per round and let them count how many times they can hit the target. This is a good warm-up exercise that forces the children to seek out good positions on the wall so they are able to throw accurately.

 The children can start in corners where it is easier to find positions that allow them to let go with both of their hands. As they progress, they can have a go at more advanced positions.

PASS IT ON

Have the children spread out on the wall, about one metre apart. Whoever's furthest to the left is given an object that is to be passed on to the next child to the right. The object is then passed on from child to child all the way to the right, and then back again.

 To make it more challenging, the children can spread further apart so that the object has to be thrown.

LIMBO
Have the children traverse a wall with a lot of holds while you're holding a broom handle against the wall for the children to climb under without

touching the broom or the ground. The shorter the climber, the easier it is, so this is an exercise which can be extra fun if you participate yourself, because nothing is more fun for kids than being better than their coach! To make it extra challenging you can assign multiple coaches to hold brooms at different heights to make an obstacle course on the wall.

💡 **Try using a hula hoop for the children to climb through.**

OCTOPUS

Have the children get established on the wall with both hands on a good hold and only one foot on a foothold. They should now try to touch as many holds as they can with their other foot for 15 to 30 seconds, before switching feet. Have them work in pairs, so that they can help each other count.

Positive handholds will allow them to move their hips away from the wall which will require less flexibility, but more strength, for placing their feet on holds which are up high or far to the side.

COLLECT THEM ALL

In advance of the session, tape notes to holds all over the wall; now have the children collect them. They are only allowed to collect one note at a time and they have to place them in a pile some way away from the wall before they can collect another.

Tape the notes in different places with varying levels of difficulty, so that everyone is challenged at their own level.

REBUS

The previous exercise can also be done as a rebus puzzle. This will then be a cooperation exercise where all the notes have either a word or a drawing, and collectively they form the answer to the rebus. The answer could be a song they have to sing or a place with a hidden prize. It's all about being imaginative.

 If the rebus puzzle is quite hard, you can number the notes to make it a little easier.

NINJA

A ninja climbs without making a single sound. This is a good exercise for working on precision climbing, and especially precision footwork. You can make this exercise into a competition, where anybody who makes a sound gets a point. Whoever has the least amount of points at the end of the round is the winner.

 Instruct the children to look at the footholds as they place their feet.

FOLLOW THE MUSIC

Play different types of music and have the children move to the tunes while they are on the wall. You don't have to lay down any rules for what type of moves they should do. Calm music usually leads to the children focusing on balance, footwork and precise movements, while faster music leads to dynamic and more physical climbing.

 Calm music can be used for a good start to the specific warm-up, or alternatively for cooling down after a physical session.

FREEZE WHEN THE MUSIC STOPS

Climb while the music is playing, but as soon as it stops everybody has to freeze where they are and be quiet. If they move or make a sound while the music isn't playing they get a point. Whoever has the least amount of points at the end of the round is the winner.

It's often easier if the music is calm, so you can start with calm music and then make it harder and harder.

NINJA WHEN THE MUSIC STOPS

Let the children climb while the music is playing, but as soon as it stops they have to continue climbing without making a sound. Those who make a sound get a point. Whoever has the least amount of points at the end of the round is the winner.

Vary between slow and fast music to create different movement tempos.

CLIMBING IN PAIRS

Split the group into pairs. Each pair has to hold hands while traversing along the wall using just one hand each. The exercise can also be performed up to the top of the bouldering wall or on top rope, as long as there are suitable routes available. Reaching the finish line will require cooperation and tactics. They have to communicate and agree on who should be moving and lay down a plan for how to reach their target.

Make up a boulder problem that *has* to be climbed in pairs. It's not so hard – just choose holds that are too far apart for one child, but where two children collectively will have enough reach. They can practise the move for a bit and then try to climb the whole problem.

CLIMBING BLIND
Have the children pair up. One child will climb blindfolded, while the other instructs their partner on where to place their hands and feet. It's

important that the instructing partner keeps the instructions short, precise and easy to understand. This is a good exercise for training balance and positioning, in addition to being a great exercise for helping the children learn how to cooperate and trust each other.

 This exercise can be performed both on the bouldering wall and on top rope, but it can be a good idea to steer clear of the tallest walls. If you're using the bouldering wall it is best to traverse close to the ground.

OBSTACLE COURSE

Use brooms, hula hoops and climbing holds to create an obstacle course on the wall for the children to climb through. They can climb over, under, around and through – the only limiting factor is your own imagination. To make it more challenging, you can tape or mark holds that are off limits. To make it even more challenging, you can tell them it's not allowed to touch any of the obstacles, or you can place objects, such as beanbags or corks, on top of holds that will fall down if they are touched. The exercise is best suited to slabs and vertical walls.

Let the children take part in planning and designing the obstacle course.

SPEED CLIMBING

This is always a hit! A speed climbing competition can be done in many ways, but in our experience it's best to use a short wall with auto-belays – as coach you can then focus on recording the time instead of belaying. Alternatively, the children can climb a boulder problem three times in a row in the shortest time possible. A boulder problem can be climbed so quickly it might be difficult to time it correctly, so it might be better to count the total time for all three attempts. Choose an easy route or boulder problem so that everybody can top it, and encourage the children to improve their own time instead of getting the best overall time.

 Ensure good safety routines if using the top rope walls.

MASTERY

As a coach for children and youth groups it's important to create mastery-oriented athletes. As opposed to being result-oriented athletes, they will now be focused on their own progress, mastery and love for the sport, and not just the result of winning a competition or climbing a boulder problem or route before others. To create mastery-oriented environments and athletes it's important to reward personal progress and effort. As a coach you should not just reward the best, but also those who have improved their results compared to last time, or those who decided to give it their all even though they ended up in fifth place.

CANDY CLIMB
The classic game of placing sweets on the holds to make the children even more psyched to climb is perhaps not the healthiest and best game to play every day, but it can be a fun alternative for a Christmas or summer holiday get-together.

 Remember, climbing holds aren't clean, so only use sweets with a wrapper!

RELAY RACE

This is a good alternative to a speed climbing competition and it rewards teamwork and cooperation instead of being an individual competition. Divide the group into two teams and line them up five metres from the bouldering wall. Have them run to the wall, climb up to a certain point, jump down and run back to tag the next climber in line. You can be inventive and add in different tasks to be performed during the race.

 A relay race should be done on the bouldering wall to eliminate elements of risk from rushing up a top rope wall.

TECHNIQUE EXERCISES

ALL OF THE exercises described in chapter 1 are also suitable for children and youths, they just have to be scaled down to suit shorter climbers with less reach and smaller hands. In addition, in this section we present some new exercises as well as bringing back some familiar ones with a twist to make them more suitable for younger climbers.

BOTTLE TOPS

Tape bottle tops to the soles of the children's shoes so that only the tips of the shoes can be placed on the footholds.

This is a good exercise for training footwork since many children are sloppy when it comes to what part of the shoe they place on the footholds. This is often the result of focusing too much on their hands and the route above instead of looking at their feet as they place them on the footholds.

Perhaps they also do not realise what a disadvantage it is to place something other than the tip of the shoe on the foothold, especially on smaller edges. Therefore, start the exercise by explaining and showing how the feet can twist off the footholds as they move around on the wall unless they have been precise in their foot placements by placing the tips of their shoes on the holds.

This will be especially apparent when traversing or moving sideways using sidepulls, where we twist the body from side to side while moving on the wall.

 If you don't have any bottle tops, you can use a slippery tape and tape off the part of the shoe that shouldn't be used.

CLIMB UP AND DOWN
By downclimbing routes after reaching the top the children will be forced to look at their feet when placing them. We recommend pairing the children up, so that they can take turns belaying each other. The exercise can also be done using an auto-belay, but this is not ideal, as the auto-belay

will pull them upwards as they are trying to climb down.

 Start with easy, vertical routes well within their limit. It's much harder to downclimb than you might think.

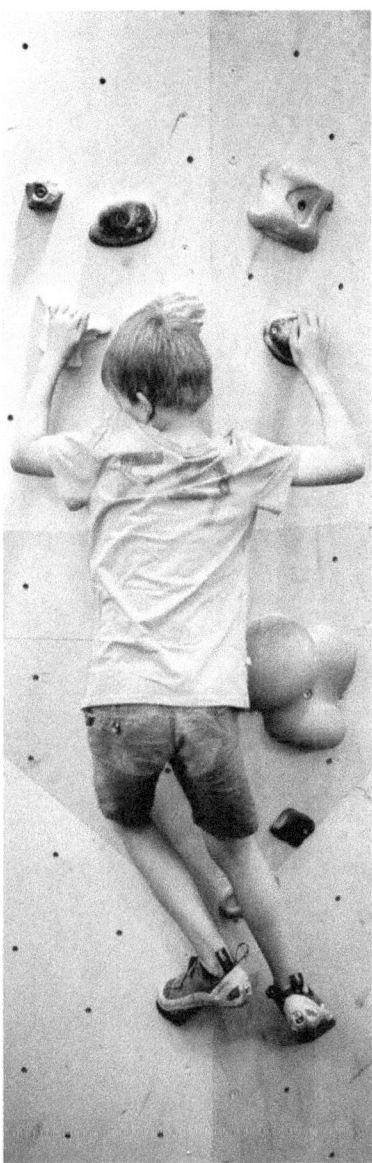

MATCHING FEET

Matching every foothold while traversing is a good way to practise this important technique. It's also a good exercise for training precision footwork and balance. Vary the wall angles and have the children experiment with footholds of different sizes and shapes.

Have the children practise different ways of matching their feet: placing one foot next to the other, sliding one foot into the same spot as they remove the other foot, and jump matching.

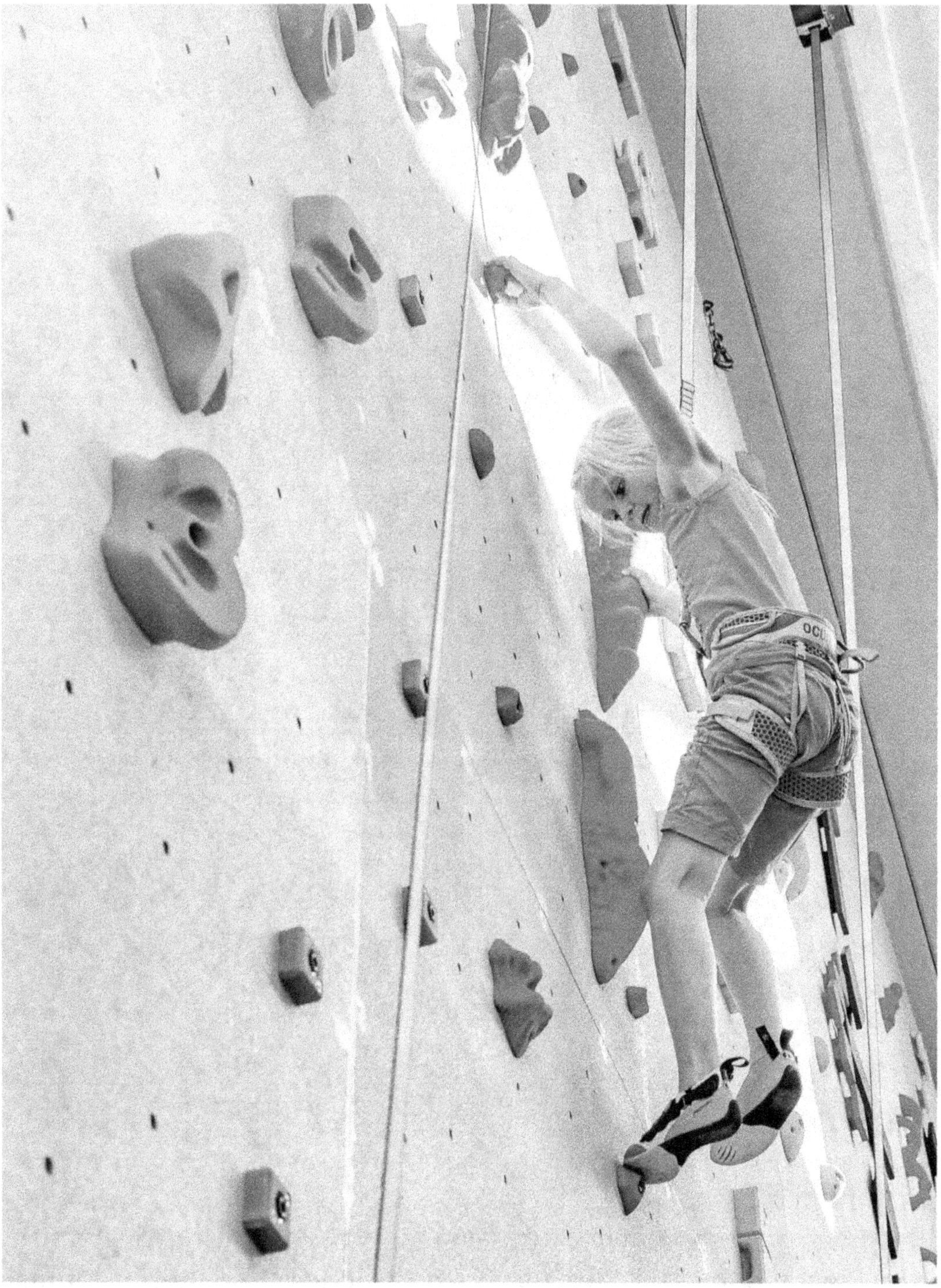
PHOTO VEGAR HERSTRØM

BABY STEPS

Doing multiple moves with our feet for every move with a hand is a good way to practise precision footwork, and it naturally makes us more aware of the importance of looking down at our feet as we're placing them. For this exercise, have the children do three foot moves for every hand move.

 Choose lines on the wall where multiple routes have been set next to or on top of one another. This allows the children to use footholds from a different route if needed.

GIANT LEAPS

Having to place our feet high is common in climbing, especially for shorter climbers, so this is an essential skill to practise. For this exercise, have the children do the exact opposite of the previous exercise – they are to climb a route with as few foot moves as possible, and for every foot move they should try to place their foot as high as possible.

To force the children into keeping their hips close to the wall, have them use only poor holds, like slopers.

QUICKDRAW ON THE HEELS

Attach quickdraws to the heel loops of the children's shoes. Have them climb as calmly as possible so that the quickdraws don't make any sound by bouncing against the wall. This requires both precise footwork and good balance as they move about on the wall.

 Give the children some time to figure things out: to begin with, it might be difficult for them to get a feel for how much the quickdraws will swing around.

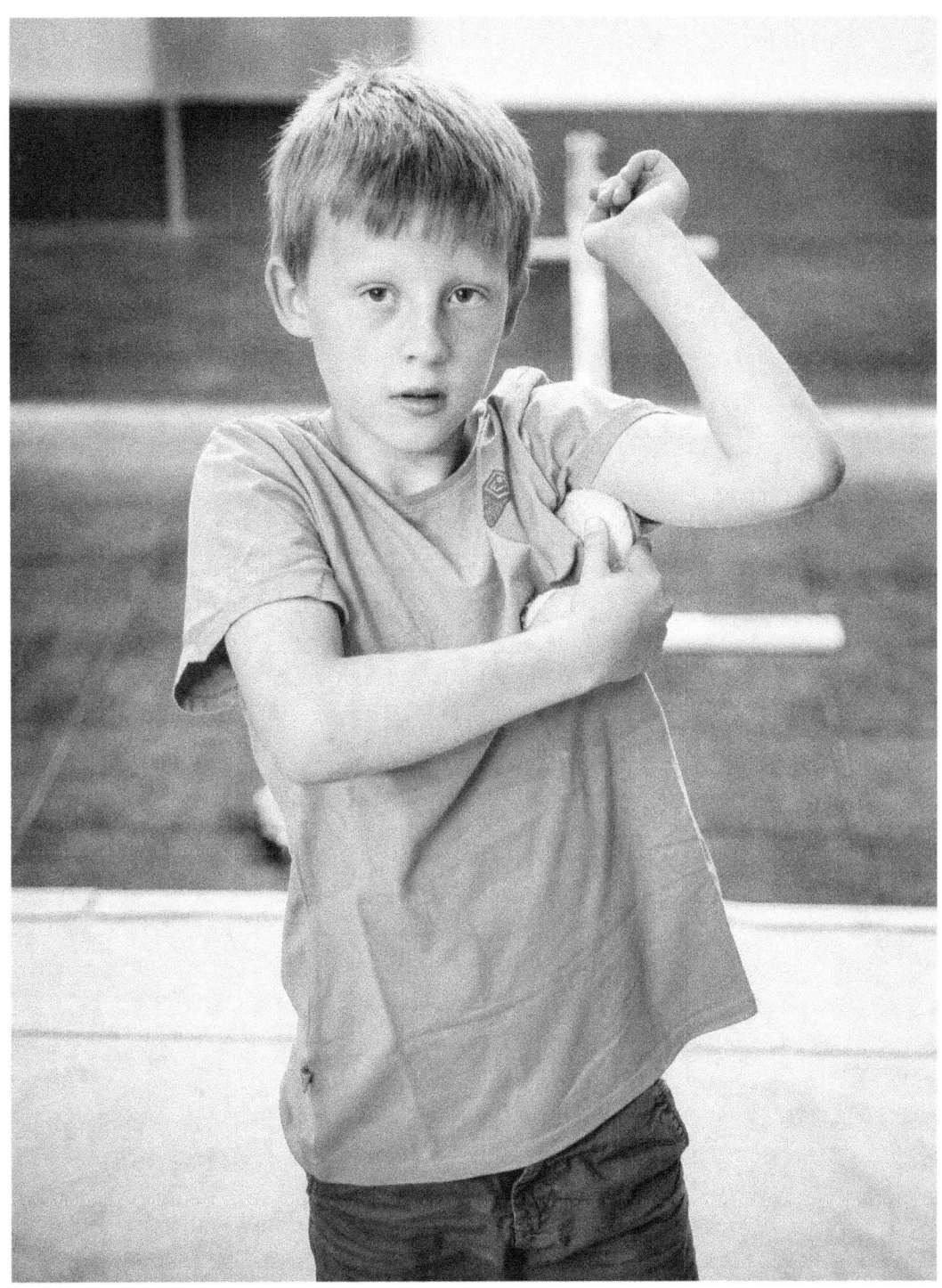

TENNIS BALL UNDER THE ARM
Have the children climb to the top of the bouldering wall or traverse an entire section of the climbing wall while holding tennis balls under their arms. This puts a significant constraint on the use of their arms, and so is a good exercise for training footwork and balance.

This exercise is best suited to vertical walls and slabs.

GUIDING

For this exercise the children are to guide each other up a route or boulder problem. One climbs, while the other points to which holds the climber is allowed to use. It's easier with free feet – meaning all footholds are allowed – on a bouldering or training wall with a lot of holds. The guide will get a better understanding of movements, and the climber gets to try moves that are different to what they might otherwise have tried.

Use a brush stick or a broom handle to point to holds.

ADD-ON

This is one of the most classic exercises in climbing. One by one, each child adds one move to the boulder problem they are climbing. The first one out defines a starting hold and climbs the first move, then the second one out climbs the first move and adds another move, climbing two moves in total. Third one out climbs the first two moves and adds a third move, and so on. The exercise helps the children remember moves, which is a very important skill in climbing. Additionally, they learn how to make up moves that work for everyone in the group, and this requires an understanding of technique and knowing each other's strengths and weaknesses. The goal is to make up a boulder problem that everyone can do.

Keep the groups relatively small, or there will be too much waiting around.

ELIMINATION

In this exercise the children are tasked with eliminating moves one by one from a boulder problem they have already climbed. Both handholds and footholds can be eliminated. Have them team up in small groups, with each climber removing one hold before taking their turn to climb.

PHOTO: VEGAR HERSTRØM

MAKING UP PROBLEMS

Naturally, as the coach, you should prepare boulder problems that are suited for the session in advance, but why not let the children do it sometimes as well? This works very well in our experience. It's fun for the children to make up problems and they learn a lot from it. Try giving them specific themes, and have them make up problems that everyone in the group can climb. When it's time for the session to begin they can show off their problems and then everyone gets to try. If the problems aren't a good fit for everyone in the group, you can add a few footholds or tweak it slightly so that everyone can benefit from climbing it.

> **BOULDERING SESSION TIPS**
> Ida-Sofie Pettersen, a Trondheim Climbing Club coach, shares how she structures the bouldering sessions: 'I usually add different challenging elements to each

problem, so that everyone can climb the same problems. Ideally, we start with an easy problem that everyone can manage within a few tries, and then I eliminate a few holds or tell them to not match any holds. This way I can keep the group together without it being too difficult or boring for anyone in the group.'

TRAVERSING

TRAVERSING IS AN excellent way to activate the whole group, and at the same time it's an opportunity to give them tasks for practising different technical elements. To make it into an interesting learning experience we suggest the following exercises.

ONE-ARMED BANDIT
For this exercise the children are only allowed to use either their right hand

or their left hand. They have to keep their other hand around their back. This is a good exercise for training balance and footwork. The exercise is best suited to slabs or vertical walls with large footholds.

HANDS ON YOUR BACK
Perhaps it's possible to traverse the slab wall without using any hands at

all? These kinds of challenges are fun and they are excellent methods for learning footwork and balance. As a coach, you have to find a suitable location for this exercise; it should be a slab with a lot of large holds and volumes big enough to be used as footholds.

SIDEPULLS

Traversing using only sidepulls is a good method for learning balance and positioning. Vertical walls are a good place to start with this exercise. To make it extra challenging, ask the children to try to avoid pinching any of the holds. As we mentioned in [chapter 1](), not using our thumbs on the holds requires better positioning of our bodies.

DOUBLES

Traversing the whole wall by only doing double dynos, big or small, is a good way for the children to familiarise themselves with dynamic climbing. Many can find this mentally challenging, so it's important to let them figure things out at their own pace. You should demonstrate in advance how to drop the hips slightly down and out from the wall to initiate the movement, before pulling up and in towards the next hold.

ROPE AROUND THE WAIST

Have the children attach a short rope around their waist with a quickdraw at the end to weigh it down; the quickdraw shouldn't be touching the floor when they are climbing. They should now traverse the wall while focusing on maintaining balance and a steady pace. If they move smoothly and correctly the quickdraw will also move smoothly and not swing back and forth.

LET THE CHILDREN FIGURE IT OUT ON THEIR OWN

In our experience, the children will learn a lot more if they figure out a move or a boulder problem on their own. You should therefore give them the tasks without too much instruction in advance; or don't give them too many corrections while they're doing the tasks. You should of course start the session by showing them what to do, and if they're learning a new technique they'll need clear instructions, but then it's important that you take a step back. It's easy to be impatient as a coach and to want to provide too much feedback too soon, because it's so obvious to you what mistakes they are making. But this can diminish their learning experience. Instead, try to give them challenges where they can learn for themselves what works and what doesn't by trial and error. This will also make it easier for them to understand what you mean when you do provide feedback.

STRENGTH TRAINING FOR CHILDREN & YOUTHS

WHETHER CHILDREN AND youths should be doing any strength training has been a subject of discussion for many years, and has been shrouded in myths. Research has now shown quite clearly that strength training is safe, and the effects are important for motor skills development, learning technique, muscular development, power, risk of injury and general health. There are no good arguments for why children and youths should not be doing strength training, and as long as the children are motivated and can receive instructions it's entirely safe to begin with structured strength training for children from the age of five or six.

We should start by defining 'children' and 'youths'. It's hard to put an exact age to these, but in research girls and boys are defined as children up to the ages of 11 and 13 respectively. Youths are defined as the period from 12 to 18 for girls, and 14 to 18 for boys. However, there can be large individual differences, and two 12-year-olds with the same chronological age can have entirely different biological ages. They can also have different training ages, meaning how many years they have been doing structured training. As coaches for children and youths these are important factors we have to consider when planning group training sessions and individual exercise programs.

There will also be significant differences between boys and girls which we have to consider when planning strength training. Throughout puberty, boys will have a stronger response to strength training because of increased levels of testosterone production and therefore increased muscle mass, and the differences in relative strength, meaning strength in relation to body weight, will thereby increase between boys and girls during this period. Girls will benefit from strength training, but will not progress at the same speed as boys, because of hormonal differences related to the production of oestrogen versus testosterone. Where boys during this period can shift their focus towards training more and harder, girls will need a slower progression in terms of load and volume. It's important that we as coaches are aware of this difference, so that we can contribute to individualising goals and controlling the load related to strength training.

WHY SHOULD CHILDREN & YOUTHS TRAIN STRENGTH?

WE WANT TO make one thing entirely clear: performance and results are not the most important reasons for beginning strength training for children and youths. Better results become more achievable if strength training is incorporated into regular training, but what we want to create are healthy, strong robust humans, who, for the rest of their lives, can reap the benefits of the training they did when they were young, and who will continue to live active lives. We can say that strong kids become strong adults, as long as they continue to train throughout their lives.

Starting from a young age our bodies respond positively to strength training. Where at first the effects in children will primarily be linked to neurological adaptation and better execution of movements, the effects through puberty will be directly linked to muscle elasticity and increased muscle mass. Together, this will result in increased muscle strength and an increased force development. This is important for the development of motor skills, for learning sport-specific techniques, and for reducing the risk of injury. All in all, strength training thereby creates robust athletes with long-term performance potential at a lower risk of injury. Additionally, we gain health benefits like increased bone density, reduced levels of fat and reduced obesity, thereby improving overall mental health and lowering the risk of lifestyle-related diseases.

Strength training does not have a negative impact on bone growth zones and will not inhibit growth like some of the myths claim. We should of course be aware of the fact that if the training dosage is too high over extended periods of time this can lead to bone damage in the growth zones, but this would be because of the excessive training dosage, and not the strength training itself. With the right methods we can argue that the risk of injury is reduced through a structured and individually adapted training program, in combination with good load control.

HOW SHOULD CHILDREN & YOUTHS TRAIN STRENGTH?

THE TIMING AND conditions for training different qualities will change throughout the development of children and youths. As mentioned, there can be large differences between children and youths of the same age, but there are still some basic principles we can adhere to.

For children, it's important that training is varied and fun. The focus should be on so-called multi-part exercises, which target larger movements and functions instead of training specific muscle groups. The training should be dynamic, not static, and the exercises should be based around using the arms and legs to carry body weight. The strength training itself should last for 15 to 20 minutes and the exercises should be physically demanding enough for there to be an effect on the nervous system. Climbing is a sport that especially focuses on the upper body, but we must make sure to also include the legs, stomach and back in the training, to stimulate the development of basic motor skills.

Here is a selection of exercises that can be done either individually or in pairs, and either alone or during organised group sessions. It's important that the children can receive instructions, and to begin with the focus should be on learning the technique of the movements. Initially, this shouldn't be a competition about who can do the most, the hardest or the fastest. Make individual adaptations and use deloading where necessary, so that the movements are executed with the proper technique. As the children get older and gain more experience with strength training, the training dosage can increase for each exercise and the internal competitiveness can be used more actively to train more, better and harder.

We recommend adding the selection of exercises as a regular part of the organised training, so that you as a coach can make individual adjustments and contribute to learning of the proper technique. These exercises do not require any additional equipment beyond the kids' own body weight, and they can be added as part of the warm-up or at the end of a session.

GOOD BASE EXERCISES TO BEGIN WITH:

PUSH-UPS
Begin by training the starting position, by keeping a straight and rigid body, without arching the back or bending at the hips. Then move on to lowering the chest deeper towards the floor.

PULL-UPS
Begin hanging from a bar and deload by either using an elastic band or by getting help from a coach so that the lift is controlled and steady.

SIT-UPS
Lie on the ground with knees bent and then lift the upper body up from the floor.

SQUATS
'Take a seat on the toilet' is usually a hit with the kids! Have them practise standing in a stable position and squatting down with their heels still in

contact with the ground.

HANGING LEG LIFTS
Hang from a bar and lift the knees up to the chest.

RECOMMENDED EXERCISES FOR PAIRS:

WHEELBARROW
One athlete gets down into the push-up position while their partner grabs their ankles and lifts their legs up from the ground. Now walk like a farmer carrying a wheelbarrow forwards, backwards and side to side.

SIT-UPS WITH A CLAP ON TOP
Both athletes lie on their backs feet facing each other with their feet together, and give each other a high five with alternating hands at the top of every sit-up.

PUSH-UPS WITH A CLAP ON TOP
Both athletes face each other in the push-up position, and give each other a high five with alternating hands. Have them vary how far to the side and how high they clap, to challenge the starting position.

ONE-LEGGED BALANCE
Both athletes face each while other standing on one leg, pressing their palms against their partner's, trying to push each other off balance.

PUSH BACK AND FORTH
Both athletes face each other, pressing their palms against their partner's. One athlete pushes the other backwards, then they switch.

Early on in puberty we can begin to add new exercises with more rapid movements, directional changes and so-called plyometric exercises. A plyometric exercise is one such as a burpee or a jump squat, where you slow down a movement before exploding back up. This will stimulate the elastic abilities of the muscles and tendons, so that they act like springs and can store and release elastic energy. We also recommend introducing the exercises that are done on the wall, as described in chapter 2. You should avoid doing the exercises on small, positive holds, and you should be prepared to make adjustments for the group you are coaching. Additionally, we recommend:

HAND SLAP PUSH-UPS

Both athletes face each other in the push-up position. The goal is to slap the 'opponent's' hands without getting slapped themselves.

PALM WRESTLING

Palms should be touching at all times, and the goal is to wrestle the 'opponent' out of a marked area or down to the ground.

BURPEES

Start in the push-up position. Do a quick push-up, then jump with arms above the head before returning to the push-up position.

QUICK PULL-UPS

Do pull-ups as quickly as possible, preferably using an elastic band to deload.

JUMP TO TWO-HANDED LOCK-OFFS

Jump from the ground to a bar, landing with the elbows bent at different angles. This can be done in combination with burpees.

TIC-TAC

Hang from two good holds. Choose three holds at different heights on each side of the body and place a foot on each hold, one by one, while returning to the starting position every time.

BODY WEIGHT AND LOADING

Body weight increases during puberty through an increase in muscle mass and fat, and this increase is different for every athlete. It's important that we maintain a dialogue with our athletes regarding this, as an increase in body weight will increase the load on the muscles, tendons and joints. In periods of rapid growth, we have to individualise the training and perhaps reduce the load for a period, so that the body can adapt to the new weight. This is especially important for finger strength training, where even just a few kilos of increased body weight can result in a significant increase in load on finger joints and on the muscle-tendon apparatus of the fingers.

Jump to lock-off.

Tic-tac.

Hand slap push-ups can be done both as a warm-up and as strength training. When the athletes can do the exercise with proper technique and in control, you can add competitive elements like trying to get the most slaps possible in 30 seconds.

During puberty, strength training will gradually start to resemble the strength training we do as adults, focusing more on muscle growth and increased strength in more specific movement patterns. We should carry with us the principles of individualising the training to everyone's level and training age, and be conscious of the fact that the way to go is to train the individual in different ways, adapted to their needs and development level. Boys, especially, will increase their muscle mass during puberty, and many of the gender-related differences in strength are related to the differences in muscle mass. Increased muscle mass and further neurological development will collectively lead to an increase in force development and stronger athletes. A thoroughly fit and strong youth will be at a lower risk of injury and be at an advantage when it comes to enduring a gradual increase in training load and learning increasingly difficult techniques. It's natural to actively use the exercises for strength and power on the wall in the training. Additionally, we recommend beginning with some isolated exercises.

DEADHANGS

Choose different holds and grip positions, for example half crimp on deep edges, three finger pockets, or an open-handed grip on slopey half domes. Maintain an 'active' hanging position, meaning the shoulders are pulled down and the elbows are angled in towards the centre. Hang for 15 to 20 seconds in this position with a margin of 3 to 5 seconds per hang. Repeat three to four sets with a 2- to 3-minute rest in between.

APPENDIX TO FINGER TRAINING

In *The Climbing Bible* we categorically discouraged deadhang training for young climbers. Here we want to modify this statement to make it slightly more nuanced: we still recommend being very careful with specific finger training for younger athletes whose fingers have not yet finished growing, but there are methods that open up the possibility for conducting finger training in a safe and controlled manner.

If we were to discourage deadhangs, we would also have to discourage climbing and bouldering, as the load on the fingers is lower for deadhang training conducted in this way than it is for regular climbing and bouldering sessions.

Controlled strength training for the fingers, incorporated into a sensible training programme, will contribute to an increase in finger strength through safer training methods than hard, finger-intensive climbing and bouldering sessions. In this way, the training can help to reduce the risk of sustaining finger injuries at a later stage. Research findings from other sports also show that structured strength training helps to reduce the risk of injury.

We still discourage campus board training and a singular focus on finger-intensive climbing and bouldering, and we recommend that young climbers vary their training to become as well-rounded and complete as possible. We also recommend that athletes, coaches and parents take any finger-related symptoms seriously, and to undergo medical examination if necessary, so that the training can be adjusted.

ONE-HANDED LOCK-OFFS

As with deadhangs, we can use hang time as a target for the training. This way we can deload as necessary to ensure the lock-off is executed in a technically correct way and in control, and still reap the benefits of strength training. We recommend training at different angles in the elbow, from 90 degrees to almost straight, with a hang time of up to 15 seconds, and a 3- to 5-second margin for every hang. Repeat three to four sets with a 2- to 3-minute rest in between.

PHOTO: JARL GÅSVÆR
Sigrid Baumberger and Ida Baardsen climbing Svolværgeita, Lofoten, Norway

Remember, it's OK to take a break to just enjoy life and the surroundings after a long day out, or after a hard training session. Here's Kasper Fjeldstad Christophersen taking a breather during a round of exploring in the magical forest of Fontainebleau, France.

www.ingramcontent.com/pod-product-compliance
Lightning Source LLC
Chambersburg PA
CBHW081615100526
44590CB00021B/3455